Build the Business That Loves YOU Back
The PEACE Strategy

Build the Business That Loves YOU Back
The PEACE Strategy

A CLEAR PATH TO PROFIT, BOUNDARIES, AND EASE FOR WOMEN BALANCING A LOT AND BUILDING WHAT MATTERS

KAYLA CALDWELL

Copyright © 2025 by Kayla Caldwell

All rights reserved. No part of this publication may be reproduced, distributed or transmitted in any form or by any means, including photocopying, recording, or other electronic or mechanical methods, without the prior written permission of the author, except in the case of brief quotations embodied in critical reviews and certain other noncommercial uses permitted by copyright law. For permission requests, write to the author, addressed "Attention: Permissions Coordinator," at the email address below.

Author Name Kayla Caldwell
Author Email Address kayla@kcvirtualbookkeeping.com
Author's website https://kcvirtualbookkeeping.com/

Build the Business that Loves You Back, Kayla Caldwell—1st ed.

TESTIMONIALS

"Before working with Kayla, I'll be honest, my numbers felt overwhelming. But she actually made me *excited* about my money again! She helped me break down every dollar coming into my business and give it a purpose in a customized way, which completely shifted the way I approach money energetics. With her guidance, I set up a bank account system that supports this flow automatically, and the clarity it brought was game-changing. I even hired Kayla to support some of my own clients, because what she teaches is *that* powerful. Her PEACE Strategy™ truly helps you build a business that feels aligned, profitable, and supportive of your real life."

Amanda Riffee, Certified Expansion & Empowerment Coach

"Working with [Kayla] has truly transformed the way I approach my business and money. [Kayla's] guidance around aligning business decisions with my values has given me clarity and confidence—not just in my goals, but in *how* I achieve them. [Kayla is] kind and incorporates the human aspect of business into all you do. I find myself planning with both peace of mind and fresh energy, while feeling assured that my business is sustainable for the long term."

Bridget Grace, Awesome Blossom Floral Design Owner

"Working with Kayla has allowed me to focus on other business areas, while knowing my finances are taken care of. Kayla has a way of simplifying topics that seem complex and making them approachable to business owners."

Molly Nutt, Acorn Digital Strategy

"Kayla has completely shifted my money mindset when it comes to putting ME and my family first. I started my business for FREEDOM, and this is exactly what she helps bring you back to."

Sasha Canady, Speaker & Founder of HERHAUS

"Kayla helped me gain the knowledge and confidence to manage my small business finances by being intentional about where my money is going.

More importantly, I have an action plan on how to reach my financial goals and still have the personal life and flexibility I desire.

The PEACE Strategy™ makes it possible to have both!"

Lindsay Bradley, MBA, CAPM, Founder & CEO, Guided Arrows

FORWARD

At the start of 2025, I declared: *This is the year I finally master my business finances.*

But I had no idea where to begin. On top of that, I was carrying serious trust issues from past experiences with bookkeepers and accountants. I wondered if I would ever find someone who actually cared.

Then I found Kayla.

From our first call, I knew it was going to be different. She didn't make me feel behind or broken.

She didn't talk over me or make assumptions. She listened to my goals, my values, my fears.

For the first time, I felt like someone got it, got the ups and downs and stress of running a business without a clue about finances, got *me*.

Working with Kayla has changed the way I feel about my finances. I'm tracking numbers and navigating spreadsheets like a boss bitch. I finally feel clear and confident when making money decisions.

I love Kayla's approach to Profit First and sustainable growth. She has helped me build a system that makes sense not only for my business, but also for my life. Her book recs, Profit First workbook, and mindset shifts? Game-changers! I've grown as a business owner, yes, but also as a person. I trust myself more. I make clearer decisions. I actually *look forward* to checking my finances and spreadsheets. Who even am I?!

If you've ever felt overwhelmed, behind, or just kind of frozen when it comes to your finances, then this book is for you. *The PEACE Strategy*^{TM} is part system, part sanity-saver. Think of it as financial clarity with a side of compassion.

Kayla's the real deal. If you're lucky enough to have her in your corner, everything gets clearer. And better.

Laura Van Antwerp
Founder & CEO of Your Sober Pal LLC
Bestselling author | Public Speaker | Wilderness Guide | Social Media Influencer

For my husband and my son —

You are the reason I chose PEACE.

You are the reason I built a business that puts family first.

This book exists because I wanted more than hustle... I wanted *us*.

Thank you for being my greatest why, and the proof that I can lead with both purpose and love.

This isn't just a strategy.

It's our story.

I love you; you are my everything.

"Peace does not mean to be in a place where there is no noise… but to be in the midst of those things and still be calm in your heart."

— **Unknown**

CONTENTS

Testimonials 5
Forward 7
Introduction 15

1. The Hidden Cost of Hustle 23
2. Why Traditional Advice Isn't Enough 35
3. When Your Business Becomes the Boss 45
4. Overview of The PEACE Strategy™ 55
5. P is for Profit — Start Paying Yourself First (Without the Guilt) 67
6. E is for Energy — Protect Your Energy Like Profit 81
7. A is for Alignment — Design a Business That Feels as Good as It Looks ... 91
8. C is for Capacity — The Secret to Sustainable Growth 101
9. E is for Ease — Making Profit the Default 109
10. Money, PEACE, & the Ripple Effect 119
11. Common Pitfalls of The PEACE Strategy™ 127
12. Finding Your Enough—and Building Beyond It 137

Conclusion 145
References 151
Resources 153

INTRODUCTION

If I could describe any successful entrepreneur in one word, it would be resilient.

You've taught yourself to show up when it's hard, stretch your time like taffy, figure things out on the fly, and keep going—long after most people would have quit. You've poured yourself into your work because you believe in it. And yes, you've accepted that a little discomfort is part of the journey if it means creating something meaningful.

But here's the thing no one tells you: hard work alone isn't enough.

If that hard work isn't aligned with your values, it will cost you your peace, your time, and your joy—no matter how impressive the numbers look.

The revenue targets are being met. The calendar is full. The team is growing.

And yet... it still doesn't feel like enough.

Not enough breathing room.

Not enough ease. Not enough connection with who you are now—because you're not the same person who started this business.

You've grown beyond survival mode. But that next level—sustainable success that feels good on the inside as well as the outside—still feels out of reach.

This isn't because you've been doing it "wrong."

It's because you've outgrown the foundation your business was built on.

Somewhere along the way, your compass—your own values—slipped to the bottom of the bag. You've been running full speed, but in a direction that no longer matches your vision.

You don't need to work harder—you need to work in alignment with your values. That's what this book will help you do: rebuild on a foundation that fits your life, so your effort fuels you instead of drains you.

Let's be real, you didn't start your business to feel overworked and underpaid.

You started it to have options. To feel present. To finally build something that fits your life—not the other way around.

But somewhere along the way, the to-do list exploded. The hours got longer. The guilt crept in. And you started wondering:

> *"Why does it still feel this hard...even though I'm doing everything 'right'?"*

My story probably sounds a little like yours.

As a girl, I was independent and bossy. But I never imagined I would run my own business while raising a child—let alone help other small business owners find confidence and clarity in their numbers so they can build their legacy, too.

I'm a firm believer that we can hold many dreams and pivot whenever life calls us to.

It is okay for goals and values to change and evolve with you and your life. Mine did as I became a wife and a mother, and they will continue to change as our seasons do.

For me, becoming a mom clarified my priorities. For you, it might be something else: a health scare, burnout, a breakup, or just the quiet realization that your business isn't working for your life anymore. I've built my business around motherhood, because I have my son's childhood in my hands and that comes first, above all else.

Back in corporate, I was the "perfect" employee. I worked long hours, I had no boundaries, and I always put everyone else first. But when I became pregnant, everything shifted.

I knew I couldn't keep hustling for someone else's dream and be the kind of person—and mom—I wanted to be: present, peaceful, and in control of my time.

So, I quit.

With just eight hours a week during nap time, I started my bookkeeping business. Within a few months, I had replaced my husband's income and helped him relaunch his own business, too.

But the real magic didn't come from spreadsheets.

It came from **clarity**, **strategy,** and a deep sense of **peace**—because I finally understood this: hard work is only truly powerful when it's aligned with your values.

When I let go of the belief that I had to do everything to have what I wanted, I discovered something even better: I could build my dream in a way that felt good, not just looked good.

And you can, too.

I know the guilt, the overthinking, and the chronic overwhelm. I also know the desire to build something of your own without missing the moments that matter most.

This isn't about perfection or productivity hacks. It's about building a sustainable business. One that pays you, protects your energy, honors your time, and gives you the space to breathe and prioritize what matters most.

That's why I created **The PEACE Strategy™**— a five part framework to help you build a business that supports your life, not steals from it.

Not just because I'm passionate about numbers, but because I've lived the alternative. I've felt the burnout. The anxiety. The shame of wanting more, but not wanting to do more.

It's time to finally have a system where you are allowed to work less and earn more, you are allowed to ask for help, and you are allowed to build a business that actually supports you and your legacy.

It's time to make a change.

Because what has gotten you here, won't get you there.

And when **we feel safe with money, we feel powerful in every area of our lives.**

That's where the PEACE Strategy™ comes in—a rhythm and a clear path, not a rigid rulebook. It's the structure you've been missing, and it's designed to support both your profit and your peace.

Here's the foundation we will build together throughout this book:

- **P is for Profit** – A cash flow system that pays you first and consistently.
- **E is for Energy** – Your time and vitality are a currency. Let's protect them.
- **A is for Alignment** – If it doesn't match your values, it doesn't belong.
- **C is for Capacity** – What are you actually available for? Let's honor your bandwidth.
- **E is for Ease** – Hustle isn't the only way. Peace and flow are possible AND powerful.

Each pillar is designed to help you shift from survival mode to sustainable success. Yes, we'll talk numbers and strategy, but I promise it'll bring more peace and more profit, without sacrificing one for the other.

You'll start seeing money and time through a new lens. You'll develop the systems and confidence to love every aspect of business, even the "hard parts."

By the end of the book, you'll have a practical, doable plan to:

- Pay yourself consistently
- Work more aligned hours
- Stop overextending
- Make peace with how you earn and spend your money
- Build a business that finally loves you back.

Wherever you are right now… you belong here.

Maybe you're curious.
Maybe you're tired.
Maybe you've tried other systems before and still feel like you're falling short.

Whether you're already in business or just dreaming of leaving corporate, this book will help you build something rooted in peace, not pressure.

You're not behind. You're just ready.

Ready to take control of your profit.

Ready to build a business around your life.

Ready to do things differently with peace, purpose, and profits at the center.

You don't need another cookie-cutter strategy that ignores your reality.

You need the strategy that finally honors it.

This book was written with women in mind because that's my story, my lived experience, and the lens I coach through. But the principles inside apply to anyone building a business grounded in clarity, purpose, and intentional growth.

That's what the PEACE Strategy™ is about.

So, let's start building the business your life has been waiting for. One that pays you without guilt, sets boundaries without burnout, and finally feels safe to sustain.

One that finally loves you back.

I'm so glad you're here, and I can't wait to walk this journey together.

Let's begin.

Your PEACE Strategy™ in Action

This book isn't about giving you more to do. It's about helping you find more clarity, peace, and confidence, one thoughtful step at a time.

At the end of each chapter, you'll find two elements to help you embody the PEACE Strategy™.

Reflection Box

These short prompts invite you to pause, notice the feelings and thoughts that surface, and connect the content to your own business and life. They're designed to spark clarity and uncover patterns you may not have seen before.

Pause & Practice

After reflecting, you'll move into a simple, grounded action step, one that supports embodiment without pressure. Think of it as a micro-shift you can make today, not a massive overhaul. These steps are where the real transformation will happen.

You don't and won't need to do them all. Do the ones that you need.

But when you do pause and practice, you create a space for lasting change.

And remember, when your seasons or goals change, you can always return to each of these exercises to reevaluate your PEACE Strategy™.

CHAPTER 1

The Hidden Cost of Hustle

"Success at the cost of your peace is too expensive."

You've already worked hard for what you have—and maybe you've even outpaced the foundation you built it on. But hustle has a hidden cost, one I didn't see until it caught me off guard.

The Wake-Up Call

The buzz of my phone jolted me awake. I had only fallen asleep a few hours earlier after a late-night news shift. Now, another breaking story needed me back at the station.

I rubbed my eyes, yesterday's makeup still clinging on, and piled on more dry shampoo. No time to enjoy my coffee, barely time to change. Just another day, starting all over again.

My contract said I had to go.

My body whispered, *you can't keep doing this.*

I wanted to say no, but I didn't even know what that would look like.

I was always available but never truly present—not at work, not at home, not even with myself.

I was out of alignment.

That was the moment I realized hustle had taken more from me than it ever gave. I was starting to hate the life I had built.

TV Dreams and Nonstop Work

Most of my life, I thought I'd be a broadcast meteorologist—yes, the weather reporter on TV.

And that's exactly what I did.

After high school, I went straight to San Jose State University and earned a Bachelor of Science degree in meteorology with a minor in broadcast journalism. I was even one class short of a math minor.

In college, I juggled a full class schedule, three part-time jobs, and summer internships all across the country.

After graduation, I moved across the country again to become a multimedia journalist and weekend meteorologist. I worked 50 to 60 hour weeks, constantly on call, turning two or three stories a day. It was nonstop.

Eventually, I was promoted to morning meteorologist for the 5am and 12pm shows. It meant another cross country move and waking up at 2am every day. It took a toll, emotionally and physically. Not to mention, I never found my people at that station, and the viewer criticism hit hard.

So, I bought myself out of my contract with a 60 days notice.

The Corporate Hustle

With just a weekend in between gigs, I moved another 400 miles and started a job in property management.

Within 11 months, I had two major promotions while planning a wedding. On paper, I was thriving. Behind the scenes, I was covering shifts, working long hours, and still… never stopping.

Another year, another promotion. More money and more pressure to cover it all to keep everything going.

I missed family events and milestones. I kept climbing the ladder, even as the ground beneath me felt less and less stable. I only stopped when I was too sick to work.

I was stretched thin, constantly proving I could carry more. Hustle had become my identity, and I was losing myself in someone else's dream.

I didn't know then that just a few years later, I'd be running a business that paid me more than that job ever did—and left me free for school pick-up, coffee dates, and slow mornings.

A Turning Point

Then, unexpectedly, I got pregnant. Our world completely shifted. We knew we didn't want this life for our child.

I told my husband, "It's my turn." He launched his personal training business, hoping clients and the money would come quickly.

"We had a plan and God had other ideas."

Two weeks after our baby was born, the COVID pandemic shutdown went into effect. Gyms closed. Plans for our livelihood completely unraveled.

I battled postpartum depression and anxiety as I thought about having to go back to work and missing my son growing up. Not to mention, my job was very different from when I left it, and childcare was non-existent.

We had to pivot, and suddenly, the dreams we thought were a year away needed to become our reality now.

Motherhood was my turning point. But maybe for you, it was burnout, a loss, or that quiet knowing that something had to change. Whatever it was, that moment matters. If your moment of truth hasn't come yet, that's okay. This chapter is a compass, not a stopwatch.

In the middle of postpartum fog, uncertainty, and a world turned upside down, we found ourselves at a crossroads.

We could stay still, hope things would change, or take a bold step toward something new without guarantees. So, we chose to move forward, one small, uncertain step at a time.

When my son was just four months old, we moved to Reno, where gyms were open. My husband found full-time work, and I stayed home with our son, but I knew I needed something that felt like mine.

From doing our taxes, I'd already seen how much my husband struggled with his numbers, and I knew he couldn't be the only entrepreneur who did. So, I enrolled in a bookkeeping course, curious if this could become something more than just a personal solution.

I was right.

Four months later, I replaced his salary with my "little" bookkeeping business. So, he left his job and relaunched his business.

Today, five years in, we both run thriving businesses. Neither of us works 40-hour weeks, and we're there for school pick-up, drop-off, and every milestone in between.

It's not always perfect. During tax season, I work more hours and I rely more on my support system. And some of those days, I still wonder, *Did I leave my 9–5 just to work 24/7?*

But then I remember why I chose this path in the first place.

I'm a mom first.

Because I shaped my business around the time and energy I actually have, I know it's profitable. Not just in dollars but in how it supports the life I am here to lead.

If you're reading this and thinking, "But I don't have kids"—this chapter is still for you.

Hustle culture doesn't discriminate.

The pressure to do more, be more, and keep all the plates spinning shows up in a hundred different ways: through work, relationships, caregiving, ambition, or simply trying to meet impossible expectations.

Your story matters here, too.

The Unspoken Pressure

*"We've been told we can do it all.
But that doesn't mean we should."*

We've all heard the questions—sometimes out loud, sometimes in our own thoughts:

- Why isn't dinner on the table?
- Why are you still working?
- Why isn't the laundry folded?
- Can't you just take care of it all?

These expectations are heavy. Just because we can do it all doesn't mean we have to.

We can ask and hire for help, make more money, work less, and still thrive and be present without permission.

Even with kids, chaos, and all the moving pieces, we can create a business that fits our lives, not one that forces us to fit into it.

> *"She didn't pause the dream; she brought her kids with her"*
> *—Made for Mothers*

Burnout Isn't Just About Work—It's About Everything You Hold

Burnout doesn't come only from your business.

It's the weight of what no one sees: the meal planning, school drop-offs, emotional check-ins, partnership dynamics, caregiving, and the constant mental load.

Many entrepreneurs aren't just building businesses; they're also caretaking partners, raising kids, supporting aging parents, and being the default decision-maker at home.

According to a Harvard Business Review study, nearly one in four entrepreneurs report feeling burned out—and that number likely underestimates how many push through without saying so out loud.[1]

---

[1] Garton, Eric. "What Makes Entrepreneurs Burn Out." Harvard Business Review, April 18, 2018. https://hbr.org/2018/04/what-makes-entrepreneurs-burn-out

This isn't just personal—it's systemic. You were never meant to carry it all, much less shoulder it on your own.

We didn't start our businesses to be busy. We started them for freedom.

Hustle can have its place when it's serving your values—but unchecked, it takes from your time, peace, and presence.

Hustle keeps you reacting instead of leading.

You might notice it in the quiet questions:

- "Did I just miss another important moment for a win that didn't even feel that great?"
- "Am I letting money—or fear—dictate how I spend my time?"
- "When did I start feeling so disconnected from the people I love?"

The deeper cost of burnout is the mindset it creates:

- "I have to do this, or no one will."
- "I can't stop."
- "There's no other way."

Burnout masks itself as commitment, but true commitment includes rest. Your worth is not measured by your hustle.

Rest isn't a reward—it's the strategy.

It's okay for things to be done, not perfect. It's okay to go slow.

Because when you're building for approval instead of alignment, everything becomes draining.

Time to Reclaim Your Peace

The version of me who was waking up at 2:00am to forecast weather on live TV—running on fumes and caffeine—couldn't imagine the life I have now.

Today, my business supports summer breaks, school drop-offs, and my peace. It didn't happen overnight, but every choice to move away from hustle and toward alignment brought me here.

And I want that same transformation for you.

You can hustle, but let it be in service of what matters most.

> *Don't build for their approval at the cost of your own peace.*

With alignment, you can:

- Build a business that honors your energy.
- Create a paycheck beyond your dreams.
- Design a life that includes rest, joy, and growth.

Just remember:

> *Money doesn't heal burnout— it masks it.*

You need to know what you actually want so you can develop a plan for your money and systems that actually support your real life.

It's not about doing more…it's about doing what matters, with support and clarity.

That's how you build the business that finally loves you back.

> **Reflection Box**
>
> This is your space to pause and be honest with yourself—no pressure, no judgment. These prompts are here to help you get clear on what's working, what's not, and what you want to shift. Let it be gentle. Let it be yours.
>
> Use these prompts to gently explore your current season. Grab a journal, a voice note app, or just sit with a cup of tea and think it through:
>
> - Are you hustling only because you think you should?
> - When was the last time you felt truly peaceful in your business?
> - What's one small change you're ready to make that could shift everything?
> - How would it feel to build your workday around your life—not the other way around?

Pause & Practice

The power is in the practice—not the size of the shift.

Imagine this...

You wake up without panic in your chest. Your calendar reflects your values. You finish work and still have energy to play, rest, and connect. Your business fuels your life—not drains it. You're present. Profitable. Peaceful.

You don't have to burn out to prove you're shining.

This isn't a fantasy. It's possible—and it starts with honoring your energy, your season, and your definition of success.

Let's make peace practical.

Choose one tiny shift this week to help your business serve your life—not steal from it. Start where you are, and keep it simple:

- **Create a No List.** Write down 1–3 things you're no longer available for.
- **Design Your End of Day Routine.** End your workday with one peaceful habit that signals it's time to rest.
- **Protect One Hour.** Block one hour this week for you—guilt-free.

Peace is built in micro-moments, not massive overhauls.

Next up: Why Traditional Advice Isn't Enough—because we're not building businesses in a vacuum. We're juggling life, kids, and big dreams. Let's explore how to build a business that truly fits you—your values, your rhythm, and your definition of enough.

CHAPTER 2

Why Traditional Advice Isn't Enough

"Everyone says 'just raise your rates,' but that's not the whole story."

If you've ever sat at your kitchen table late at night—laptop open, lost on what's next, listening to yet another podcast promising "the secret to success"—and wondered why it's not working for you, I want you to know: **Traditional Advice Isn't Enough.**

It might have gotten you this far, but now you need something different—because the foundation you've been building wasn't designed with *you* and your real life in mind.

You're not lazy, uncommitted, or "playing small." You're navigating client calls between school drop-offs, crafting content while folding laundry, and trying to build a meaningful business without losing yourself in the process.

Traditional business advice rarely accounts for that reality—or for your *capacity*. It assumes unlimited time, energy, and childcare. And when you don't have those, it's easy to feel like you're the problem.

You're not.

If It's Not Working, It's Not You

Let's talk about why so much business advice falls flat—and how you can build a business that actually fits *your* life.

When you entered the online business space, you were probably met with a flood of tips:

- Just raise your rates.
- Outsource what doesn't light you up.
- Batch your content.
- Hire a Virtual Assistant.
- Work smarter, not harder.

Sounds easy, right? Except…

What if you're still not paying yourself consistently?

What if your workday is built around school drop-offs, toddler tantrums, and laundry loads?

What if your energy is limited—not from laziness, but because you're carrying a lot?

There's no shame in any of this.

I used to think something was wrong with me because I couldn't make those strategies stick. I tried the hustle. I signed up for the webinars. I believed that if I just "did it right," I could build a profitable business and still be fully present for my son.

But here's the truth: we weren't handed a playbook for how to price, plan, or protect our peace. We're learning it on the fly. And the usual business rules? They weren't made for caregivers, creatives, or anyone building from the heart instead of the hustle.

The Broken Promises of Business Advice

You've heard the typical tips. Maybe you've even tried them. But for so many solopreneurs, these one-size-fits-all strategies fall flat in real life:

- **Hustle harder:** You've already maxed out. More hours aren't the answer.
- **Outsource it:** Sounds great—until you realize you don't have the systems or budget.
- **Raise your rates**: Not helpful if you're not selling your current offer.
- **Reinvest everything**: Not if you actually need a paycheck (and you do).

Sometimes, one or two of these tips help. But advice that ignores your season, your values, or your actual capacity? That's where things break down—and where we need to start.

Signs Traditional Advice Isn't Serving You:

- You feel more guilt than momentum when trying to follow tips that don't match your reality.
- You've hired help or invested in support—only to end up more stressed or confused.
- You find yourself asking, "Is my strategy wrong… or is this advice just not made for me right now?"
- Common mantras like "just raise your rates" or "just outsource it" sound good but feel risky, unrealistic, or misaligned.
- The business world often feels like it wasn't built for people juggling caregiving, chronic illness, mental health, or solo survival.

You are not alone.

Even small things can feel big. Like trying to get out the door on time. There's always a missing water bottle, an unexpected spill, or a last-minute shoe change.

So yeah, calls might happen in the car, during nap time, or while your kiddo's at practice—or while you're managing appointments, caregiving, or your own recovery.

And that's not unprofessional. That's reality.

The Moment I Knew It Didn't Fit

I was lucky to learn business basics from another mom during the pandemic, who told me I could build my business during nap time.

That wisdom stuck—because whether your business is built during nap time or in the cracks between client work and caregiving, your time boundaries can be a *superpower*.

So I leaned into that wisdom.

I figured out what my family needed, calculated how many clients I needed, and found them—around nap schedules and part-time childcare.

But even with that solid foundation, it was hard. I was used to doing it all. Asking for help felt painful. And I still made decisions from scarcity, undercharged, took on any client, and worked too many hours. I girl-bossed too hard.

Eventually, I hired help and put my son in part-time daycare. But even then, I knew I had to build small and strong, so I didn't miss the moments that mattered.

That was the moment I realized: I wasn't failing. I was trying to follow advice that didn't fit the season I was in.

Client Story: What She Really Needed

One of my clients had done *everything* the online gurus told her—freebie, funnel, email sequence—but she was discouraged and still not paying herself.

Within two months of working together, she was paying herself consistently and had stopped working weekends for the first time ever.

How? We didn't pile on more strategies. We simplified. She narrowed her offers, raised her prices, built a proper cashflow system, and carved out buffer time in her week.

She hadn't been failing. She had just built a business that looked good on the outside but didn't support her life.

The strategy didn't change her worth or her values—it revealed them.

And her story isn't unique—neither is the solution.

The Real Reason It Doesn't Work: Capacity and Care

Whether you're a parent, caregiver, or simply managing a full life, *emotional labor* is often invisible but very real.

And the toll isn't just emotional; it's measurable.

- According to a recent report led by Intel, 72% of founders suffer from mental health challenges, and more than a third report struggling with anxiety.[2] When you're building a business while carrying an invisible load, that's not surprising.

We carry a mental and emotional load at home and at work. And that load shrinks our capacity.

This affects how we price, plan, delegate, and deliver—so we need boundaries, better delegation, and pricing that truly reflects our time, energy, and season of life.

We need systems and clients that understand our life comes first.

Reframing Success: What We Actually Want

We want to be paid. We want to be present. We want to make a difference—without losing ourselves in the process.

To you, success might look like:

- A six or seven-figure year—or even just $25k, if that's what fully supports your family in this season.
- Hiring a nanny to handle pickup—or showing up to coach your kid's t-ball team yourself.
- Working three days a week—or taking Fridays off to head outside.

Whatever your definition, this is what I like to call your *Enough*.

The idea was inspired by Morgan Housel's *The Psychology of Money*, where he shares how knowing your personal "enough" is one of the most powerful drivers of financial clarity.

I've shaped that concept for building a life-led business by asking:

What's enough time?
Enough income?
Enough energy?

Not someone else's definition of success—*yours*.

> *Your enough is personal. Your success is unique. Profit isn't just about numbers; it's about peace.*

In the corporate world, we were shamed for putting our families first. But here? You are celebrated!

You get to define success on your own terms. You get to:

- Build a business that aligns with your life.
- Find clients who respect your priorities.
- Grow in ways that honor your energy.

You don't need permission. You just need the right fit and a foundation that supports your version of enough.

> **Reflection Box**
>
> Take a few minutes with these prompts. Journal, talk them out, or just sit with them:
>
> - What part of traditional advice has felt the most out of touch for you?
> - How does your current season of life shape what you need from your business?
> - What would it mean to build a business that supports your capacity—not just your ambition? (Consider what would happen in an emergency—the impact of caregiving, chronic health challenges, or carrying the full emotional load on your own.)

Pause & Practice

Imagine you are having coffee or tea with your future self. Ask her what's changed. What are you doing in your business? What are you doing for fun? Where are you living? Who are you spending time with? How did you get there?

Now, take just one small step to start honoring that version of you—because clarity doesn't come from overthinking. It comes from taking aligned action, one choice at a time.

Choose one:

- **Audit the Advice.** Write down one business "should" you've outgrown or never resonated with. Cross it out. Replace it with a truth that fits your season.

- **Simplify One Offer or System.** Look at your calendar, offers, or workflows. What's more complex than it needs to be? Trim, pause, or streamline one thing.

- **Define Enough.** Choose a revenue goal or schedule that actually supports your current season—not someone else's standard. What does enough look like for you right now?

Traditional advice isn't broken. It's just not built for us. That's why what you're building now—on your own terms—is revolutionary.

Next up: When the Business You Built Becomes the Boss—a chapter that dives into what happens when hustle becomes your default and freedom starts slipping through your fingers. Together, we'll explore how to recognize the warning signs, reclaim your time, and realign your business with the life you actually want.

CHAPTER 3

When Your Business Becomes the Boss

"I didn't leave one boss just to answer to a hundred smaller ones."

If you've ever found yourself still working, dishes still in the sink, laundry untouched, and your child already asleep without you... this chapter is for you.

If you've ever told yourself "just one more email," only to miss the sunset walk you promised your partner or your dog, this chapter is for you.

If you've ever sat at your desk, building your dream, while silently wondering if it's costing you the very life you wanted to build it for, this chapter is especially for you.

We don't talk enough about the quiet resentment that builds when the business you love starts taking more than it gives. You're the CEO, the team, the bookkeeper, the copywriter—you wear all the hats. The hours keep increasing, the joy keeps decreasing, and the guilt? Always there.

And often, it doesn't happen overnight. It creeps in slowly. At first, it's a missed bedtime or a skipped lunch. Then, it's a whole weekend where you can't unplug. Eventually, you look around and realize that the business you built to create freedom now steals all your capacity.

Realizing the dream you built is draining you can feel like grief. But it's also a beginning.

"I didn't leave corporate to lose my weekends, too."

That sentence echoed in my head. It wasn't just frustration—it was a wake-up call.

I had built this business for freedom, but I found myself recreating the same overstretched version of my old corporate life.

And I see other entrepreneurs doing exactly the same, all the time.

Brilliant, soulful entrepreneurs building businesses from the ground up, only to wake up one day and feel like they traded one version of burnout for another.

Instead of a boss setting the schedule, it's clients.

Instead of coworkers overloading you, it's your own sense of duty and ambition.

And while profit matters, it should never come at the expense of your peace.

Boundaries Are Not Optional

We sacrifice our own time to keep clients happy, stay visible, and stay ahead. But when boundaries blur, burnout follows.

You might recognize it as:

- Saying yes to one more project.
- Giving away too much for free.
- Letting work spill into weekends, again.
- Ignoring that voice inside whispering, "I can't keep doing this."

We don't just feel exhausted—we feel invisible. And when our contributions are minimized or unnoticed, that quiet resentment builds. We stop asking for help. We convince ourselves it's easier to do it all alone.

But that's not leadership. That's survival.

And surviving isn't the goal. Thriving is.

It's time to build stronger boundaries so your business stops taking more than it gives. Because the longer we operate without them, the more we gradually destroy the very things we say matter most: profit, presence, peace, joy, and connection.

You weren't meant to be everything to everyone. Not in business, and not in life.

You don't get paid to simply sustain—you get paid to grow. And growth only happens when you protect the time, energy, and focus that make it possible.

You're Not Wrong for Wanting Peace AND Profit

A client once told me, "Everyone says I should increase my prices."

When I asked what she'd do with the extra income, if she did increase her prices, she paused, then said, "Honestly? I just want my weekends back."

It clicked. It's not about choosing between peace and profit. It's about designing a business that gives you both.

We've been taught to choose between making money *and* protecting your peace, but they can and should coexist.

We've been fed a myth that hustle is the only path to success. That more clients, more hours, more effort equals more value. But what if your value isn't tied to how much you do, but how clearly and powerfully you show up?

What if working less didn't mean less success but more impact?

Because a sustainable business fuels your life and doesn't consume it.

From Guilt to Permission: Rewriting the Rules

When I was in Kelly Ruta's Subconscious Millionaire program, one of the many take-aways for me was that I did not need permission.

We're taught to seek permission before making bold moves. But this is your business. Your dream.

Give Yourself Permission

If you're waiting for someone to tell you it's okay to...

- Raise your rates
- Say no
- Step back for a season

Here it is: you have my permission.

But more importantly—I want you to start giving *yourself* permission:

- To build a business that protects your peace.
- To slow down without fear that it will fall apart.
- To define success on your own terms.
- To let go, move forward, and lead from values—not urgency.

Validation won't build you the life you want. But giving yourself permission—that is where it begins.

The "Double Your Rates" Wake-Up Call

In one of my toughest seasons, I heard: "You can afford to lose half your clients, if you double your rates."

Raising my rates always stirred up fear and self-doubt, but this reframe changed everything.

It made me realize the problem wasn't my pricing alone—it was my entire approach to capacity.

It made me re-evaluate:

- Who we were serving.
- What we were charging.
- Whether we were delivering our best work.

I didn't let go of half my clients overnight, but I did raise my rates with confidence, even knowing we could lose clients in the process.

That confidence didn't just come from spreadsheets or benchmarks. It came from alignment.

From clarity. From the realization that working more hours wasn't making us better; it was making us bitter.

By choosing value over volume, we created breathing room. For our clients, our team, and our families. This happened about three years into my business, during a season when I realized I couldn't keep running on empty. We restructured our offers, raised our rates, and finally stopped saying yes to everything.

And in that space, new opportunities appeared.

Higher-value partnerships looked like fewer, more aligned clients who shared our values and respected our boundaries. These were clients willing to collaborate long-term, pay for strategic insight (not just execution), and refer others who were a great fit.

Sometimes, that also meant rehoming clients—intentionally transitioning them to another provider who was a better fit for their needs or budget. Rehoming isn't failure; it's a capacity and alignment strategy that serves everyone. It frees your time and energy for the clients who energize you, while ensuring the others still receive great care from someone aligned to serve them.

That shift—fewer but better-aligned clients, plus the courage to rehome those who weren't a match—allowed us to step into deeper, more fulfilling work. And best of all, it gave us freedom to step away without fear.

Peace isn't just a feeling. It's the result of decisions, systems, and boundaries that support how you want to live.

> **Reflection Box**
>
> Take a moment to check in without judgment.
> - Where is your business taking more from you than it's giving?
> - Which clients, projects, or habits drain you most?
> - If you rehomed or restructured just one of them, what would open up?

> You don't need to have the full plan. You just need to be honest with yourself.

Pause & Practice

Give yourself permission to:

- Say no without an apology or long explanation.
- End your workday on time at least once this week.
- Remove one energy drain from your plate—by automating, delegating, or rehoming it.

Notice how it feels in your body when you do this. Do you feel lighter, calmer, maybe even a little more like yourself?

This is where sustainability starts, not with scale, but with self-trust.

The business you built doesn't have to keep taking more than it gives.

It can start giving back when you build it with clarity, compassion, and choice.

And you're not wrong for wanting more—more simplicity, more alignment, more time to breathe. You're not failing. You're just operating with a blueprint that never accounted for *you*.

But that can change.

You don't need to burn it all down. You just need a new way forward; one that's built on values, sustainability, and vision.

That's where the PEACE Strategy™ comes in.

In the next chapter, I'll walk you through the framework I created not just to fix the symptoms, but to rebuild the foundation. One that puts your life, your energy, and your freedom at the center.

Not a list of rules, but a rhythm to return to when things feel off.

CHAPTER 4

Overview of The PEACE Strategy™

*"I just want a plan that works with my life—
not against it."*

By now, you might be feeling more clear about what's been holding you back—and more ready than ever to do something about it.

You're ambitious. You're capable. But you've been trying to run your business with systems that weren't built for the way you live, work, and lead. And no matter how many tips or "proven strategies" you've tried, something is still missing.

What you want isn't a shortcut. It's a way forward—a clear, adaptable plan that honors your time, your energy, and your values.

Because you don't just want a business that pays the bills. You want a business that gives you more—more peace, more breathing room, more alignment with the life you're building.

What if your business could be a source of energy instead of exhaustion? What if it could support your life instead of competing with it?

Here's the truth: you don't have to wait for someone to hand you permission, a blueprint, or the "right" timing.

You are the architect. And starting now, you get to build differently.

That's exactly why I created the PEACE Strategy™.

A Framework that Honors Real Life

I've always loved learning. I devour books, binge podcasts, and curate my feed for growth (with the occasional cute dog video, because balance).

But most of what's out there? It's incomplete—especially for women building businesses around their actual lives. I've picked up golden nuggets from brilliant mentors, but no single path ever felt fully right or enough.

And honestly? I don't always agree with the big-name entrepreneurs. There's often a catch. Rarely baby steps. And definitely no room for real life schedules.

So, I simplified. I built a way to grow without burning out—a system that blends money-savvy strategy, life-first business design, and the kind of mindset shifts that actually stick.

I wanted something repeatable. Adaptable. Flexible enough to work for you in *your* current season, without demanding you become someone you're not.

Because you don't need *my* exact path. You need a framework that works with YOU—*your* values, *your* goals, and *your* reality.

That's what the PEACE Strategy™ is: a flexible framework for women, like us, who want to build a life-led business that actually works—and meets you exactly where you are—in the season you're in now.

> **Reflection Box**
>
> Before we dive into each letter, pause—not to fix anything, but to claim your role in what comes next.
>
> This isn't about waiting for clarity to arrive. It's about creating it.
>
> You already have the insight you need—you've just been buried under advice that didn't fit.
>
> Now's your moment to notice what you want to shift, so you can build on purpose.

Now, let's explore each pillar, not as rules to master, but as guideposts to help you realign with your values and vision.

The PEACE Strategy:

P → **Profit**

E → **Energy**

A → **Alignment**

C → **Capacity**

E → **Ease**

The  Strategy™

P is for Profit

"I just want to feel like I'm making money, not barely scraping by."

Profit isn't just revenue.

It's paying yourself. Planning ahead. Pricing based on reality, not guilt.

It's the systems that stop the undercharging cycle and help you actually understand where your money is going.

Profit is what helps you own a business—not a job.

Profit isn't just about big launches or hitting seven figures. It's about consistently paying yourself, taking a break without panicking, and finally seeing the fruits of your labor.

You're not just building a business. You're feeding a family. Paying bills. Carrying a mental load that few people see. Just plain old adulting.

Profit matters because your work deserves to sustain you, not just look good on paper.

> What would change in your life if you consistently paid yourself first?

 is for Energy

"I'm exhausted and I don't know if I can keep doing this."

You can have all the systems in the world, but if you're running on fumes, none of it will stick.

Energy isn't just sleep. It's your emotional bandwidth. Your decision fatigue. The quiet drain of holding everything together.

Ignore it, and you risk resenting the very business you built.

Protecting your energy means designing a business that fuels you instead of draining you.

> What would change in your life if you started scheduling rest for yourself?

 is for Alignment

"I'm doing all the things, but none of it feels quite right."

Misalignment shows up quietly: draining clients, off-brand offers, and strategies that feel wrong in your gut.

When we chase what we "should" do, we disconnect from what we actually want.

Alignment isn't fluff; it's the foundation.

Because when your work reflects your values, everything gets clearer. And when it doesn't? Burnout begins.

> What would change in your life if you worked with your dream clients?

 is for Capacity

"I'm booked out, burnt out, and still broke."

Capacity isn't just time. It's energy, support, and mental space.

Most of us override our real limits to prove we can keep up.

But ignoring your capacity doesn't make you more committed. It makes you more at risk.

Honoring your bandwidth creates space for smart decisions and sustainable growth.

> What would change in your life if you could work less, guilt-free?

 is for Ease

"I don't want everything to feel so hard anymore."

We've been taught to glorify the struggle, as if hard means worthy.

But ease isn't laziness. It's clarity, flow, and systems that support you.

Offers that sell because they're rooted in what you do best.

You're allowed to want a business that feels good to run.

You're allowed to let it be easier.

> What if one task you dread could happen automatically, every single time?

When you honor your energy, you increase your capacity. When you align your offers, profit follows with more ease.

> **Reflection Box**
>
> This is your moment to pause. Release the shame. Be gentle with yourself.
>
> Let your answers be honest, without judgment.
> - Which of the five pillars (Profit, Energy, Alignment, Capacity, Ease) feels most off right now?
> - Which pillar feels the easiest to strengthen first?

> - What would shift if you gave that one area more attention this month?
> - If I trusted my own way fully, here's what I might try next...
>
> This isn't about getting it "right." It's about hearing yourself clearly.

Pause & Practice

You don't have to master every pillar right now—and you don't have to prove anything to anyone.

Choose one area that feels most urgent or exciting, and decide how you'll support it this week.

- If it's **Profit**, decide how you'll pay yourself first or adjust your pricing with intention.
- If it's **Energy**, block time for rest and protect it like your best client meeting.
- If it's **Alignment**, choose one offer or client to realign with what feels right.
- If it's **Capacity**, intentionally clear space—say no, pause, or delegate.
- If it's **Ease**, pick one task to automate, simplify, or hand off.

You're not ticking boxes—you're taking ownership.

Peace starts when your choices match your values, one decision at a time.

You Don't Have to Master It All

You don't have to rush. Peace happens one aligned step at a time.

This framework isn't about doing it perfectly.

It's about building differently—with peace at the center. Think of it as a compass you can return to again and again, depending on your season.

In the next chapters, we'll walk through each letter of the PEACE Strategy™ and uncover what's been holding you back. Start with the pillar that will give you the most relief and the clearest win.

For many women I work with, that's **Profit**.

Because your peace starts with getting paid.

OVERVIEW OF THE PEACE STRATEGY™ | 65

Want to Put This Into Action Faster?

If reading feels like a lot right now, I've got you covered.

Grab your free PEACE & Profit Starter Kit—with a guided workbook, podcast-style audio lessons, and plug-and-play templates—so you can start applying this strategy in real life today.

thepeacestrategy.com

Scan the QR code or head to *thepeacestrategy.com* to get instant access.

Because sometimes, clarity clicks faster when you have it right in front of you.

CHAPTER 5

P is for Profit – Start Paying Yourself First (Without the Guilt)

"Profit isn't greedy. It's sustainable."

Stop Stealing from Your Future

"Stop buying coffee, and you'll afford a house."

Advice like that makes us feel like we are the problem—like our dreams are just one skipped latte away.

Yeah, right.

Maybe that advice works in theory, but where I live, $3,000 doesn't get you a down payment, and my morning coffee? It's how I survive the toddler meltdowns, the puppies, the clients, the team, and everything in between.

If your coffee is the thing that keeps you going, buy the damn coffee. Just make sure you budget for it.

This chapter isn't about deprivation. It's about intention.

Every dollar you earn and spend should reflect the life you want to build. That's what I call your Peace Point—and it starts with paying yourself first.

Somewhere along the way, many of us were taught that keeping the profits for ourselves meant we were greedy. That spending made us "bad with money."

But here's the truth: money may not grow on trees, but it can grow in your business—and you can attract the resources you need, whether that's a new client, a referral, or another opportunity arriving in ways you couldn't have planned, exactly when you need it.

Profit isn't about clinging tighter or hustling harder. It's about being a wise steward of what comes in, trusting that there is enough, and leaving space for more to flow in.

If money talk makes your stomach turn or your eyes glaze over… you're not alone. But what if your numbers could be your compass and not your critic?

Here's what I want you to know:

> Profit creates options. Options create peace. Peace builds a life you love.

Profit isn't selfish. It's *smart*.

The Profit First Shift

I discovered Profit First at a time when I was exhausted—undercharging, overdelivering, and constantly wondering where the money went. I felt like I was always just trying to stay afloat.

But once I started applying this system, it wasn't just my bank balance that changed—it was my mindset. I stopped seeing money as something to chase or fear and started seeing it as a tool I could trust.

Mike Michalowicz's cash flow system, *Profit First,* changed the game for me. The idea is simple, we take the traditional Formula:

Sales - Expenses = Profit

And we flip it for the **Profit First Formula,** and those of us without an accountant brain:

Sales - Profit = Expenses

Same math, different mindset.

Instead of waiting to see what's "left over," you pay yourself first and run your business on the remainder. It forces creativity, encourages thoughtful spending, and centers *you* in your business.

This chapter could easily be a book of its own—and thankfully, it already exists. I highly recommend **Profit First by Mike Michalowicz** if you want to dive deeper. For now, my goal is to give you a simplified starting point, so you can begin to understand your numbers with clarity and confidence.

Here's how it works:

Step 1: Set Up the Core Bank Accounts

We'll be setting up these separate bank accounts specifically for your business. It's essential to keep your business and personal finances separate, not just for clarity, but to protect your peace of mind and support smart decision-making. Not to mention it protects personal assets from your business liability.

Start with **five key accounts**:

- **Income** — where all your revenue funnels in.
- **Profit** — your bonus, your celebration fund.
- **Taxes** — for Uncle Sam (yes, we plan for him!).
- **Owner's Pay** — This pays *you*.
- **Operating Expenses** — what's left to run the business.

If this feels like a lot right now, start small. In addition to your main business checking account, open just two accounts: one for Profit and one for Taxes. Begin by setting aside just 1% of your income.

Think of it like giving your money a set of labeled jars. Profit is your celebration jar. Taxes is your "peace of mind" jar. The rest stays in your main account for everything else.

Suddenly, instead of wondering where it all went, you know exactly what's what—and you feel more in control with every deposit.

> **Pro tip:** Use high-yield savings accounts so your money works for you while it sits there.

This isn't just about profit; it's about sustainable profitability that honors your life.

Step 2: Start Simple

If this feels like a lot, *breathe*. You don't have to do it all today.

Try this first:

- Move **1%** of every sale into Profit.
- Move **5%** into Taxes.

So, if you make $100:

- $1 → Profit
- $5 → Taxes
- $94 stays in your regular checking for now.

Plan to make these transfers at least twice a month. Personally, I like to do them every Monday, and I grab myself a muffin to reward myself. So I call it my Money Muffin Monday date.

As you grow more confident, we'll divide further.

Step 3: Discover Your Next Step

Look at last year's numbers. (If you don't have those, look at the average over the last three months.) If you made $100,000 and paid yourself $20,000, that's **20% Owner's Pay**.

So for now, pay yourself 20% of each sale—and allocate what's left to expenses.

Example:

- 1% → Profit
- 5% → Taxes
- 20% → Owner's Pay
- 74% → Operating Expenses

Not ideal, but a *great* place to start.

Step 4: Find Your Peace Point

Your Peace Point is the monthly income you need to comfortably cover your real-life responsibilities without stress. It's not just a number; it's a reflection of your values and a foundation for making aligned decisions instead of anxious ones. Defining this early gives you a target to work toward as you restructure your finances with intention.

Before you run numbers, create a calm space. Light a candle, pour your favorite drink, and block 30 minutes for a *clarity date* with yourself. The more intention you bring to this, the more clarity you'll receive in return.

Let's take an honest, judgment-free look at what your life and business actually cost.

Start by listing *every* expense—daily, weekly, monthly, quarterly, and annually—for both your business and personal life. Keep the lists separate so you can see each clearly.

If an expense varies month to month, take the average from the past three months and use that as your monthly cost.

Then, do a gentle audit:

- What no longer serves you?
- What still aligns with your current values and priorities?

If an expense brings up shame or guilt, pause. Evaluate. (Most likely, it's time to let it go.)

Essential costs stay. But everything else? ALWAYS up for negotiation.

Once you know this, you can:

- Cut the excess.
- Adjust your pricing.
- Stop stealing from yourself.

Your Peace Point isn't just a number; it's a reflection of your values. When your income supports your real life, you make decisions from alignment, not anxiety.

Step 5: Roll It Out—Slowly

Every 90 days, adjust your percentages slightly to get closer to your peace point. One percent can make all the difference.

Start:

- 1% Profit
- 5% Taxes
- 20% Owner's Pay
- 74% Operating Expenses

Next Quarter:

- 2% Profit
- 5% Taxes
- 25% Owner's Pay
- 68% Expenses

Build over time. Let this be a plan you grow into, not a sprint.

> A helpful rule of thumb: Aim to save and keep 1 to 3 months of operating expenses in one account at all times. Think of it as your business's breathing room, not just for emergencies, but for PEACE.

If you're not sure where to start, I have a **free Profit First Assessment and Rollout Plan Generator with an instructional video** available on our website. You can also explore the **Profit First app** for additional support if you like your tech.

Profit Is a Celebration

The businesses that last are not the ones that hustle nonstop. They are the ones that pause to celebrate. Celebration is part of sustainability.

Use Profit money to reward yourself every quarter or every year with:

- A latte
- A massage
- A vacation
- Paying down debt, but remember to reserve a little for something joyful. You deserve to celebrate along the way!

Profit shows up in your books *and* in your life.

My clients have used profit to:

- Pay for honeymoons
- Buy wedding rings
- Take family trips
- Buy their ski passes
- Buy their backpacking accessories

> The only time we ever use Profit money for anything other than celebrating your hard work is if your business carries debt, whether it's student loans, credit card balances, or startup expenses. We still take one to 50 percent of it for yourself and the rest to pay down debt.
>
> Or maybe you add a Debt account. Keep a simple debt tracker and commit to a small portion of your monthly cash flow (2–5%) toward paying it down. Even small steps create momentum and ease.

Make It Yours

When in doubt, add an account.

Customize as needed:

- Open a **payroll account** if you have a team
- Use **high-yield savings accounts** for Profit and Taxes
- Consider using a credit card for expenses and paying it off monthly to earn points

Real Client, Real Clarity

Need proof that this can grow with you? Let me introduce you to one of my favorite success stories:

One of my clients, a thriving floral designer, fell in love with Profit First. At first, she was skeptical: how could managing five accounts possibly make life *easier*? But now? She has over **30 Profit First accounts**, each aligned to a specific need: fresh flowers, education, rent, taxes, and even a "one day" account to help her fund her future dreams.

Her Profit First system isn't rigid; it's personal, fluid, and aligned to what matters most to her.

She knows exactly how much to pay herself, how much to reinvest, and how far in advance she can plan for both opportunities and downtime. Her business doesn't just *run*, it thrives. Why? Because she's anchored in clarity, not chaos.

This system became her **confidence engine.**

> **Investors & Other People's Money**
>
> Bootstrapping is a powerful starting point, but it's not the only path.
>
> If you ever consider bringing on investors to grow your business, here's the good news: investors love Profit. When you've baked profit into your cash flow system, you can clearly show how their return will be prioritized and predictable.
>
> That said, money always comes with expectations. Before accepting outside funding, get clear on your own values, vision, and boundaries. Those should guide every decision, not the size of someone's check. If you move forward, ensure you have a solid contract and a lawyer who understands small business partnerships. Protect your PEACE and your purpose.

Final Reminder

Profit is not a dirty word.

Okay... Maybe it *feels* that way sometimes. Especially if you were raised to believe money was private, indulgent, or never meant to be shared.

But here's the truth:

Profit is your reward, your safety net, and your legacy.

It doesn't make you greedy. It makes you grounded. The more money you keep, the more peace and purpose you can create.

> **Reflection Box**
>
> - What's one old money story you're ready to rewrite?
> - What's one small profit habit you could start today?
> - How would it feel to use profit for something joyful?
> - What's your current Peace Point and how can you meet it more consistently?

Pause & Practice

Your Peace Point Planner (DIY or Done-for-You)

If you're ready to take the next step, I've got two options:

Option 1: DIY Peace Point Planner

Create your own worksheet to map your monthly income needs. Open a fresh doc or journal and list:

1. Personal Monthly Costs: Rent/mortgage, groceries, child care, insurance, etc.
2. Business Monthly Costs: Tools, subscriptions, team, taxes, etc.
3. Highlight anything that feels like a "should" vs. a "must."

4. Add it up. That's your Peace Point—the number that lets you breathe.

Option 2: The Starter Kit

If you prefer guided support and take the guesswork out of this process, my Starter Kit includes:

- A plug-and-play Peace Point Calculator
- A mini podcast series walking you through the exercises
- A journal to reflect on everything that comes up

It's designed to give you clarity now, not six months from now. You'll simply plug in your numbers, and the tools will help guide you forward.

thepeacestrategy.com

You Don't Have to Perfect Profit Overnight

Profit isn't about hustling harder or mastering every percentage today.

It's about starting where you are, creating clarity, and letting your numbers work for you—not against you.

Even small shifts can create big breathing room.

That breathing room is what allows you to focus on your most valuable resource: your energy.

Because profit fuels the business, but energy fuels you. Without it, even the most profitable business will drain you dry.

So before we chase more growth, let's focus on what matters most—protecting your energy and building a business that fuels your life as much as your bank account.

CHAPTER 6
E is for Energy – Protect Your Energy Like Profit

> *"Think of your energy like a luxury item—not everyone can afford it. Not everyone has earned the right to access it."*
> —Inspired by Taylor Swift

Last chapter, we talked about profit—the financial fuel your business needs to thrive. But profit alone won't protect you from burnout. Money gives you options, but energy is what lets you *use* those options well. Without it, even the most profitable business will start to feel heavier and harder.

That's because energy is the quiet resource behind your creativity, your clarity, and your ability to serve well. When it's protected, your business flows. When it's depleted, everything feels like pushing through mud.

As moms, entrepreneurs, and humans trying to balance… well, everything… we often joke that we wish we had the same energy as our kids. I mean, where does it even come from?

But ask them to do chores and—poof—it's gone.

We're not so different. Some tasks light us up. Others drain us the moment we see them on our calendar.

And knowing the difference? That's the key to building a business that's profitable *and* sustainable.

Energy is a Currency

We often talk about budgeting our time and our money. But **energy**? That's the real fuel behind everything.

When your energy is running low, even simple things feel heavy. Decision-making, creativity, showing up online—it all gets harder. But when your energy is protected, your business flows.

You make better choices, connect more meaningfully, and serve more powerfully.

Your energy is a **currency**. And it deserves to be budgeted just like your money.

Just like your Peace Point gives you financial clarity, your Energy Budget helps you spend your time and focus where it counts.

Because profit without energy is like money without time—you're still trapped.

What Fuels You, What Drains You

Let's get practical. Ask yourself:

- What fuels me?
- What drains me?

Drains might include:

- Endless meetings
- Lack of boundaries
- Overdelivering to your clients
- Mindless scrolling

Boosters might look like:

- Slow mornings
- Walks outside
- Creative projects
- Intentional time blocks for deep work

Pause & Practice

The Energy Audit

This week, try this simple 3-step process:

1. **Track your tasks.** As you go through each day, jot down what you're doing and how each task makes you feel: energized, neutral, or drained.

2. **Label each one.** Mark each task as either "Fueling" or "Draining" based on your energy response.
3. **Take action.** For draining tasks, ask: can I automate, delegate, or delete this? For energizing ones, ask: how can I protect or expand this?

These patterns will show you where your energy is going and where it's asking to be redirected.

At the end of the week, review your notes:

- What tasks made you dread your day?
- Which ones gave you spark?

For the draining tasks, consider:

- Can I outsource this & trade it for a more profitable task?
- Can I automate or delete it?
- Is it time to pivot my offer?
- Is it actually making me more money?

For the energizing tasks:

- How can I do more of this?
- Does this reflect where I bring the most value to my clients?
- How can I center my offers around these tasks?

Even the best offer can fail if it depletes you. And if you're too tired to implement it, even the best idea won't go far.

Ready to bring your energy patterns to life? Sketch your ideal week with high and low energy zones. Color-coding helps turn insight into routine.

The Peaceful Energy Week

Morning High Focus Energy	Best for: CEO work, strategy, money, &	Mon- Fri 9:00-11:00 AM	Money dates, content creation, client strategy calls
Midday Lower Energy + Life Admin	Best for: Light client work, admin, email, or rest	Mon- Fri 11:30 AM-1:30 PM	Lunch, walk, checking inbox, client catch-ups, batching
Afternoon Family and Flex Time	Best for: Kid pickup, play, or low-stakes biz tasks	Mon- Fri 2:00-4:00 PM	Family focus, errands, unplugged time
Evening Creative or Rest Reboot	Best for: Optional creativity or total rest	Mon- Fri 7:00-9:00 PM	Brainstorming, journaling, or quiet time
Weekend Flow	Saturday: Joy + Presence → Farmer's market, family time, unplugged rest Sunday: Reset + Prep → Time blocking, meal prep, profit reflection		

Honor Your Rhythms

This is where we ditch the burnout.

You don't have to operate like a robot to be successful. In fact, tuning into your natural rhythms helps you structure your work around **when you're most focused** and **when you need rest**.

That's what creates sustainable momentum.

When I began scheduling around my energy and not the clock, I was more productive, more present, and more profitable. I could work *less* and get *more* done.

Try tracking your energy:
- What time of day do you feel most productive?
- When do you usually crash?
- What feels heavy?
- What feels light?

> For women, especially, tracking your cycle with your tasks and calendar can reveal surprising clarity.

Once you see your pattern, start building around it:

- Schedule creative work during high-energy windows.
- Block off downtime when you know your energy naturally dips, whether that's midweek, midafternoon, or a certain time of the month.
- Batch harder tasks when your focus is strongest.

You deserve a business that honors your energy, not one that drains it.

Because just like financial enough gives you peace, energetic enough gives you margin—the space to rest, recalibrate, and keep showing up sustainably.

Let Energy Guide Your Sales

How you market your business and how it makes you feel matters. The strategies you choose should not only attract the right clients but also feel aligned, energizing, and sustainable for *you*.

If big networking events energize you and consistently bring in leads, lean into them.

If intimate masterminds or workshops feel more aligned, build your calendar around those instead.

One of my clients used this exact lens with her team. She realized she was assigning tasks based on job titles, not energy. Her social media manager dreaded analytics, but lit up when creating story-driven content. Her admin was drained by scheduling client calls, but loved organizing systems and SOPs. So, we restructured roles to match strengths and energy.

The result? The social media manager's content became more magnetic, pulling in dream clients. The admin streamlined workflows that saved everyone hours each week. Not only did revenue grow, but the team felt more ownership and joy in their roles. By letting each person focus on what energized them, she turned a group of individuals into true team players—more productive, more profitable, and more aligned.

When your sales strategy—and your team's roles—match your energy, it becomes sustainable. And sustainability is where real success lives.

We can't avoid all the draining tasks. But we *can* design businesses that protect our best energy and turn it into our biggest ROI.

Energy-aligned sales strategies might include:

- Weekly coworking calls
- One-on-one consults
- Monthly newsletters
- Collaborations with aligned peers

Choose what lights you up, not what drains you dry.

You won't always get this perfect, and that's okay. Energy isn't static. This is about noticing patterns, not controlling every minute.

> **Reflection Box**
> - What's one task you're no longer available to do?
> - When during your day (or week) do you feel most alive?
> - What's one shift you can make this week to protect your energy?
> - Where could you realign your team's roles with their natural energy?
> - Where on your calendar could you block creative time or recovery blocks this week?
> - What's one 'no' you can practice to protect your energy?

Pause & Practice

Quick Win

- Block 1–2 hours next week for **creative time** and **rest**.
- Actually, put it on your calendar—right now.

Protect that space like you would a client call. Remember, every 'no' creates space for a more powerful 'yes'!

Because you're the most important employee your business will ever have: when you thrive, so does your business!

When your energy is honored, everyone connected to you feels it. Your family notices your presence. Your clients feel the difference in how you show up. Your team thrives under steadier leadership. Protecting your energy isn't selfish—it's one of the most generous things you can do as a CEO.

When your energy flows, profit follows, peace deepens, and life gets lighter.

We started this journey by uncovering what's been holding you back, then built a foundation with **Profit** and now **Energy**. Next up: **A is for Alignment**—because once your profit is protected and your energy is guarded, the real magic happens. That's when your offers, clients, and calendar line up with your values—and your business starts to feel like it's truly *yours* again.

CHAPTER 7

A is for Alignment – Design a Business That Feels as Good as It Looks

"Just because it sells doesn't mean it serves you."

You've got the clients.

The invoices are paid on time.

You're even getting eight hours of sleep most nights.

And yet... you're dragging yourself to the laptop.

That little spark you used to feel before a project? Gone.

You keep telling yourself you should be grateful—after all, this is what you worked so hard for.

But here's the thing: you can have profit and energy on paper, and still feel empty if your work isn't aligned with what matters most to you.

Profit gives you stability. Energy keeps you going. But alignment? That's what makes it all feel worth it.

Profit without alignment still leads to burnout, and misaligned work will drain your energy no matter how much money or energy you have. Alignment is the bridge that makes both last—and what keeps you loving the business you've built.

What Alignment Really Means

I don't know about you, but all my life I heard, *"Do what you love and the money will follow."* For a long time, I thought that was cute advice for other people—not me.

But when I started working for myself, spending more time with my family, and helping other women do the same, something clicked. And sure enough—the money followed.

The trouble is, we don't always build our businesses on what we love. Sometimes we say yes to what we *should* do, or what someone else told us would "work," and we end up miserable.

Here's what I say to that: **Stop shoulding all over yourself.**

As I have mentioned in Chapter 2, one of my biggest takeaways from *The Psychology of Money* by Morgan Housel is: **you have to define your own "enough."**

Not what you *think* you should want. Not what looks impressive on social media. Not even what once felt aspirational and now just feels like pressure.

"Enough" is the space where contentment meets clarity and where your true priorities have room to lead.

When you define your own enough, you stop chasing someone else's version of success and start creating a business and life that supports you, not the other way around.

Money Mindset & Alignment

We all carry money stories. And if you haven't unpacked them, they're likely running the show.

You can have the best strategy in the world, but if your mind and energy aren't aligned with it, the money won't flow.

I've taken on clients who weren't a good fit out of scarcity. I've said yes when I should have said no—and I paid for it in time, energy, and stress.

Once I started aligning my offers, pricing, and clients with my values, I stopped feeling like I had to hustle my way to worthiness. The money became easier. The work became lighter.

The Consequences of Misalignment

When your offers don't light you up…

When your systems can't support growth…

When your pricing doesn't reflect your time or value…

You end up bitter, burnt out, and disconnected from the business you built.

Sometimes misalignment doesn't show up in your calendar—it shows up in your body:

- A tightness in your chest before client calls
- Procrastinating on projects you once loved
- Secretly hoping someone cancels

Misalignment whispers before it screams.

Realigning Your Offers & Services

One client of mine was booked solid with offers she didn't even enjoy. The money was there, but the joy was gone. After revisiting her values, she shut down her biggest revenue stream—then replaced it with something new and fully aligned. She made more money and loved showing up again.

That's the power of alignment.

Realigning your offers isn't just about joy—it's about protecting your energy.

Too often, I see women underpricing because they're afraid of scaring people off.

But pricing isn't just math, it's messaging. It tells the world what you're worth and how you work best.

That's why, if hourly work is draining you, shifting to package pricing can be so powerful. It gives you more control over scope, positions you as a strategist, and lets you scale your income without scaling your hours.

When your pricing reflects your value and your bandwidth, you attract the right people. You won't be for everyone's budget, and that's the point!

Realigning Your Clients

Now, let's look at your client list. It should reflect your values, capacity, and long-term goals.

If you're dreading certain calls, overdelivering without boundaries, or feeling misaligned with a client's energy, it's time to make changes.

Small shifts can create big freedom:

- Rehome clients who are no longer aligned
- Communicate transitions clearly with kindness
- Make space for dream clients who energize you

You deserve to work with people who respect you and your boundaries.

Realigning Your Schedule

Now, let's look at your calendar.

Are you rushing through your days?
Skipping lunch?
Forgetting why you started this business in the first place?

When your schedule is crammed with back-to-back commitments, you leave no room for creativity, rest, or the things that actually make you love your work.

Refer back to your Pause & Practice Exercise in Chapter 6. Your schedule should reflect your energy patterns and your family's needs—not just the demands of your inbox.

Small changes go a long way:

- Batch similar tasks together to avoid constant mental switching.
- Add 15-minute buffers between calls so you can reset and breathe.
- Build in quiet mornings or creative Fridays to work on projects that light you up.

Your time deserves intention, not leftovers.

Realigning Your Strategy

Zooming out, let's talk about your business goals. Are they yours—or are they borrowed dreams from someone else's highlight reel?

It's so easy to scroll online and adopt someone else's version of success—a six-figure launch, a daily content calendar, a packed mastermind. It might look impressive on Instagram, but if it doesn't serve your season, that's not success. That's stress.

Your version of success will change with the season you're in, and that's okay!

Maybe this is your season to push for growth. Or maybe it's a season to protect your time and create space. Either way, alignment means letting your current values—not past ambitions or outside pressure—set the course.

Alignment isn't just clarity. It's the boundaries you set to protect what matters. This is your business. Your life. You get to choose.

> **Reflection Box**
> - What would my business look like if it fully supported my ideal lifestyle?
> - Where am I sacrificing my values for someone else's version of success?
> - If you raised your prices to reflect your value and bandwidth, what would change in the kind of clients you attract?
> - What am I ready to realign?

Pause & Practice

The Alignment Audit

Step 1: Review Your Work & Offers

List every offer, service, and recurring task in your business. You can refer back to the Energy Audit in Chapter 6. For each of these, ask:

- Does this align with my values?
- Do I enjoy it?
- Is it helping me build the life I want?

Step 2: Rank Each One

- **Love it** – energizes you and aligns with your values
- **It's fine** – neutral but necessary
- **Can't pay me enough** – drains you, misaligned, or underpriced

Step 3: Decide What to Do With Each

- For "Love it": Center these in your packages and offers.
- For "It's fine": Keep them, but consider batching, automating, or outsourcing.
- For "Can't pay me enough": Raise the price, delegate, outsource, or refer out entirely.

Step 4: Build Your Week Around Your Best Energy

- Schedule creative work during high-focus times.
- Block breaks during low-energy windows.
- Protect family time and non-negotiable personal priorities.

Step 5: Spot the Gap

The difference between what you *are* doing and what you *want* to be doing? That's your roadmap for realignment.

> **Pro Tip:** Pricing for alignment does more than cover your costs—it attracts the kind of clients who respect your boundaries and value your expertise.

Want this audit as a plug and play spreadsheet? It's waiting for you in the PEACE & Profit Starter Kit—designed to walk you through every step.

Alignment frees you to work in a way that feels natural, not forced.

It's also what helps you honor your version of enough—so your goals feel fulfilling, not just impressive.

But even the most aligned business will drain you if you push past your true limits.

That's why next, we'll talk about **Capacity**—the secret to sustainable growth. Because when your time, energy, and commitments match the season you're in, your business stops feeling like a grind and starts moving with you.

You are worthy of a business that fits you perfectly—one that honors your life, your family, and your dreams on *your* time.

CHAPTER 8

C is for Capacity – The Secret to Sustainable Growth

"It's not that you're bad at time management; you're just at capacity."

As business owners, we are constantly weighing:

Is that the right move for me right now?
Can I handle taking that on?
How many sports can my kid do without me losing it?

And, the big one: *Can I really be Superwoman?*

The answer—absolutely not.

Balance doesn't exist, and that's totally okay.

Life and business come in waves. Some seasons swell with energy and opportunity. Others pull you inward.

The goal isn't to control the tide—it's to learn your rhythm, ride it with grace, and trust in your timing.

Sometimes, it's as simple as: *not right now.*
Other times: *that's probably not going to happen for me.*

And that's not failure—that's clarity.

Clarity that lets you protect your energy and work with the tide instead of fighting it. Because even the best offers and smartest strategy can't save you if you're constantly pushing beyond your true capacity.

I used to think entrepreneurship wasn't for me. I grew up watching my parents build cash-eating monsters that never quite made it. Money came and money went. I thought the safest path was one without risk.

But here I am—building a business that's profitable, peace-giving, and family-first. And this is just the beginning.

What Capacity *Really* Means

Capacity isn't just about hours in your day—it's your full bandwidth: mental, emotional, and physical energy.

Some days, the tide is high and you have more to give. Some days, it's low and you don't. And that's normal.

One client I worked with was juggling a growing business, a toddler, and a full plate at home. On paper, she was thriving—booked solid, steady revenue. But she was waking up anxious, going to bed exhausted, and running on fumes.

Once she acknowledged that she was operating well beyond her capacity, we restructured her client load, outsourced a few draining tasks, and reclaimed hours each week. Within two months, she was more profitable *and* more peaceful.

When you operate beyond your limit everyday, things start to break—quality dips, creativity dries up, and resentment builds.

True growth starts when you *honor* your real limits and work with the tide, not against it.

Redefining Working Hours

"I know what to do; I just don't have time to do it."

Let's bust the myth that success equals 40-hour weeks. That model was never designed for women juggling business and family.

For many of my clients, 12–20 focused hours a week is all they've got. And you know what? That's enough—when you use it well.

When I started my business, I had eight hours a week. That was it. I worked during nap times and evenings. As my capacity grew, I added part-time child care and outsourced strategically.

Some seasons—like tax season—I work more. Others—like school breaks—I work less.

That's the beauty of capacity: it flexes with your life, and you can set those boundaries without guilt.

Boundaries Build Profit

Boundaries don't limit success, they expand it.

When you clarify your time and energy limits, you:

- Attract clients who respect your process
- Say no to misaligned offers
- Stay focused on high-ROI work

One of my most impactful boundaries? No client calls on Monday mornings. I used to start my week already behind frantic, reactive, and burned out by noon. Now, Monday mornings are CEO time for planning, finances, and creative focus. That single shift increased my delivery quality and gave me control of my week.

When I started saying no to what drained me, my income grew, my stress dropped, and my joy came back.

Wondering if it's time to hire?

Start by noticing what constantly drains your energy and pulls from your capacity. If you're able to outsource even 5–10 hours a month and still pay yourself, it might be time to bring in support.

I chose to hire earlier than most would recommend—not because I had it all figured out, but because my family needed me first. Buying back those hours didn't just give me time, it gave me *space to think bigger*.

Boundaries are business tools, not personal failings.

Of all the pillars in the PEACE Strategy™, this is the one I still find myself coming back to the most. I can spot my misalignment with capacity faster now, but it's still easy for me to overextend, especially when I'm excited about what I'm building. That's why I revisit this work often. Not to get it perfect, but to stay rooted in what's real and sustainable.

> **Reflection Box**
> - Where am I consistently overextending myself?
> - What boundary would feel empowering to put in place?
> - How would my business feel if I honored my real capacity?

Pause & Practice

If cutting back feels scary, you are not alone. High-capacity women often confuse doing less with doing worse. But honoring your limits is leadership, not laziness.

The Capacity Audit

Step 1: Audit Your Week

- Look at your past week. How many *real* hours did you work?
- Be honest, what time was focused, undistracted, and productive?

Step 2: Name Your Season

- What's your life like right now? New baby? School-age kids? Aging parents?
- What feels sustainable *this* season?

Remember, your capacity isn't fixed. It shifts with your season, your health, and your support system. That's not failure. That's wisdom.

Step 3: Map Your Capacity

On a sheet of paper or spreadsheet, create three columns:

Task/Category	Weely Hours Spent	Weely Hours Ideal
Client work	10	8
Marketing	5	4
Admin & Emails	6	3
CEO Time	1	3
Personal time buffer	0	2

Then, total both columns. Ask:

- Am I trying to squeeze 30 hours into a 15-hour week?
- What needs to go, shift, or wait?

Step 4: Create 3 Boundaries

- One for time (*No meetings after 2pm*)
- One for energy (*No calls on Fridays*)
- One for recovery (*Sundays are screen-free*)

Rooted, Not Rushed

Superwoman isn't the goal. Sustainability is.

Your business is meant to grow *with* you—not at your expense.
You're not behind. You're right on time.
And I am so proud of you for doing this work.

Capacity isn't just about managing time—it's about honoring your true bandwidth. Just like your Peace Point shows you what's enough financially, your capacity shows you what's enough for your time, energy, and presence.

When you honor your real limits, you protect more than yourself. Your family feels it, your team feels it, and your clients feel it. That's the ripple effect of capacity: everyone gets a calmer, more focused version of you.

And here's the gift of capacity: the space you create isn't just for rest—it's what makes smarter systems possible.

Because once you know how much time you truly have, you can design your business to move with the tide, not against it.

Capacity clears the space. Ease fills it with structure. Systems are what protect your peace, lighten your load, and make profit your default—not your afterthought.

CHAPTER 9

E is for Ease – Making Profit the Default

"Ease doesn't mean effortless. It means being intentional."

I cannot tell you how many times I have gotten on the phone with my biz bestie and blurted out, "I'm so tired of swimming upstream! Can I just burn this down? Nothing is working right?!"

If you've ever had that moment—you're not alone.

As Codie Sanchez shared on *The Big Deal* podcast and in her book *Main Street Millionaire*, her dad once said:

> *"You aren't truly in the game unless you find yourself in the dead of the night, head in hands, sitting in the dark, with no idea what to do next."*

We've all been there. And if you haven't yet, you will—especially if you're serious about growing your business. And if you're here, I imagine you are.

Lack of ease isn't about lack of talent—it's about lack of systems and support.

Sometimes, we're too fried to learn something new.
Sometimes, we don't know how to use our tools optimally.
And sometimes, we don't even know better options exist.

But once we create systems, everything changes. You build a business that's more profitable, more resilient, and—most importantly—one that supports your life even on your hardest day.

Ease Isn't Just Tech—It's Emotional Support

Ease isn't just about tech and automation. Some of the most powerful "ease systems" are emotional ones. The Community System—the people and relationships that keep you steady when the waves get rough.

Entrepreneurship can be lonely. Your priorities shift. Your views evolve. And not everyone will get it.

Your success is deeply tied to who's in your corner—your partner, your best friend, your parents, your nanny, your biz besties. The people who step in when you need to step up in your business.

With the right support systems, you can be fully present during life's best moments without scrambling—whether it's summer with your kids or taking time off for yourself. That's not magic. That's the gift of ease.

Ease Requires Effort

Let's be clear: ease isn't magic. It's built—one intentional system, one clear boundary, one simplified process at a time.

It's not about removing effort but eliminating *wasted* effort. The kind that comes from redoing, chasing, firefighting, and spinning your wheels.

It's the hard work of setting things up once, so you don't have to keep reinventing the wheel.

Systems don't set themselves up. Boundaries don't hold themselves.

At first, it feels slower—like you're stopping to build a sturdy boat instead of just swimming—but that's what keeps you afloat when the waves get rough.

When you invest the time to create templates, document processes, and automation, you're not just saving hours. You're buying back peace of mind.

Ease isn't the absence of effort—it's the reward for intentional effort. And that reward grows as your systems do the heavy lifting for you.

But remember, systems don't always make life easier. Sometimes, they reveal where you're weakest. They show you the leaks, the bottlenecks, the places where things fall apart under pressure. That's not failure—it's clarity. Once you see the gaps, you can fix them.

And here's the bigger picture: you might not be thinking about selling your business—and that's okay. But smart systems do more than give you freedom today. They increase the long-term value of your business. Clean financials, clear SOPs, and a documented brand process make your business more resilient, more attractive, and more valuable—whether you keep it or sell it down the road.

SOPs and Safety Nets

Here's what most solopreneurs miss: SOPs aren't just for big teams. They're for everyone—even if you're a team of one.

Clear, repeatable processes make it easier to delegate when the time comes and protect your peace when you're unexpectedly out of office.

Think about it like this: if something happened and you had to hand off your client load for a week, could someone else step in easily? Could your family or a virtual assistant find what they need?

Start simple: onboarding, offboarding, invoicing, and client communication. Then, add as you go.

SOPs don't have to be complicated. A quick Google Doc or screen-recorded video can be a game-changer.

Don't forget your legal and protective systems, like contracts. A solid contract isn't just about liability; it's about clarity. It outlines expectations, boundaries, and responsibilities so you can lead with confidence and protect your peace.

Ease is where your systems start working for you, and your business finally feels lighter. It creates more space for profit, clarity, and sustainability. It's what lets you ride the waves without capsizing—because your systems act like the steady current beneath you.

Defining What Ease Looks Like for You

Ease doesn't mean lazy; it's just one more version of alignment.

It's about making intentional moves, not reactive ones.

It's working from clarity, not chaos.

Ease, on the other hand, invites you to lead with intention and step fully into your CEO role.

It can look like:

- A clear workflow that saves you time.
- Automated payments so you don't chase invoices.
- CEO days to zoom out and lead with clarity.
- AI tools that handle repetitive daily tasks.

> My philosophy for ease and accepting payments? Always make it easy for your clients to pay you—even if that means paying merchant fees. Build the 2–4% fee into your pricing. It's the cost of doing smooth business—and a write-off.

Tiny Systems That Make a Big Difference

Ease is asking: where am I still making things harder than they need to be?

Here are a few small but mighty systems that can transform how your business feels:

- Weekly money check-ins
- Profit First transfers—scheduled weekly or bi-weekly
- Automated invoicing & reminder emails
- Templates for onboarding, offboarding, and social posts
- Weekly team check-ins or huddles—short, focused updates to keep priorities aligned
- A project management dashboard so projects and deadlines are crystal clear

You can also explore using AI tools to save time, like automating client responses, drafting content outlines, or summarizing meeting notes. You don't need to be tech-savvy to get started. These tools can take work off your plate, so you can focus on what matters most.

One of my clients used to feel completely overwhelmed by her inbox. She was manually sending every onboarding email, welcome packet, and invoice. We set her up with a few basic email templates and a simple automation using her CRM, Honeybook. A week later, she messaged me and said, "I feel like I can finally breathe."

Not only did she reclaim hours each week, but she started her client relationships with confidence instead of chaos. That's the ripple effect of ease.

And remember: it's okay if this feels uncomfortable at first. Letting go of control isn't weakness—it's a CEO-level trust move.

It doesn't need to be fancy. Consistency is the secret sauce—one system at a time.

ONE SYSTEM AT A TIME TRACKER

A gentle roadmap to simplify, automate, and restore your peace.

System Focus for January
- System Name: _____
- Start Date: _____
- First Step: _____
- Progress Bar: ☐ ☐ ☐ ☐ ☐
- Celebration Note: _____

System Focus for February
- System Name: _____
- Start Date: _____
- First Step: _____
- Progress Bar: ☐ ☐ ☐ ☐ ☐
- Celebration Note: _____

System Focus for March
- System Name: _____
- Start Date: _____
- First Step: _____
- Progress Bar: ☐ ☐ ☐ ☐ ☐
- Celebration Note: _____

System Focus for April
- System Name: _____
- Start Date: _____
- First Step: _____
- Progress Bar: ☐ ☐ ☐ ☐ ☐
- Celebration Note: _____

System Focus for May
- System Name: _____
- Start Date: _____
- First Step: _____
- Progress Bar: ☐ ☐ ☐ ☐ ☐
- Celebration Note: _____

System Focus for June
- System Name: _____
- Start Date: _____
- First Step: _____
- Progress Bar: ☐ ☐ ☐ ☐ ☐
- Celebration Note: _____

System Focus for July
- System Name: _____
- Start Date: _____
- First Step: _____
- Progress Bar: ☐ ☐ ☐ ☐ ☐
- Celebration Note: _____

System Focus for August
- System Name: _____
- Start Date: _____
- First Step: _____
- Progress Bar: ☐ ☐ ☐ ☐ ☐
- Celebration Note: _____

System Focus for September
- System Name: _____
- Start Date: _____
- First Step: _____
- Progress Bar: ☐ ☐ ☐ ☐ ☐
- Celebration Note: _____

System Focus for October
- System Name: _____
- Start Date: _____
- First Step: _____
- Progress Bar: ☐ ☐ ☐ ☐ ☐
- Celebration Note: _____

System Focus for November
- System Name: _____
- Start Date: _____
- First Step: _____
- Progress Bar: ☐ ☐ ☐ ☐ ☐
- Celebration Note: _____

System Focus for December
- System Name: _____
- Start Date: _____
- First Step: _____
- Progress Bar: ☐ ☐ ☐ ☐ ☐
- Celebration Note: _____

Companion Visual: One System at a Time Tracker

Use it as a visual cue that reminds you: success comes from clarity, not chaos. One. System. At. A. Time.

> **Reflection Box**
> - Where am I overcomplicating things in my business right now?
> - What would shift if ease became my default?
> - What system could I simplify or automate this week to create more peace?
> - What task do I need to delegate with a simple SOP?

Pause and Practice

Automate just one system.

Maybe it's your bookkeeping. Whether you use QuickBooks, a spreadsheet, or a notebook, set up something easy to maintain.

Commit to 5 minutes a day or one money hour a week where you categorize your transactions.

Make it fun. Celebrate yourself with a Money Muffin Monday date. Light a candle. Put on your favorite playlist.

When one system feels solid, move to the next.

But here's the best advice I can give you: **One. System. At. A. Time.**

Give each one space to evolve. A week, a month, sometimes even three months. No rush. We're playing the long game.

Because few things are more exhausting than trying to fix one broken system while juggling three others that aren't working either.

You deserve a business that runs smoothly—one that supports you, not the other way around.

These small habits yield the biggest ROI—not just in money, but in peace. They protect your presence so you're not always catching up, but finally catching your breath.

Because when ease becomes your default, profit isn't just possible—it's inevitable.

And once each pillar of the PEACE Strategy™ is in motion, the real magic happens when you weave them together. That's where clarity deepens, calm becomes your baseline, and profit flows naturally.

In the next chapter, we'll bring it all together—so you can see not just the parts, but the bigger picture: how money, PEACE, and the ripple effect create a business (and life) you're proud to lead.

CHAPTER 10

Money, PEACE, & the Ripple Effect

"I need something that will actually stick."

You've built each piece of the PEACE Strategy™:
Profit that pays you.
Energy that sustains you.
Alignment that anchors you.
Capacity that protects you.
Ease that supports you.

Now, it's time to zoom out—because ease isn't just about systems. It's about weaving Profit, Energy, Alignment, Capacity, and Ease into one rhythm that actually lasts.

Because when the pieces align, PEACE isn't just a framework. It's a clear path to how profit becomes predictable, peace becomes sustainable, and your ripple effect begins.

Take a breath. Look at how far you've come—not just in what you've learned, but in how you've changed the way you think, feel, and lead.

You're no longer defaulting to someone else's version of success. You're releasing old rules and building a business your way—rooted in clarity, intentionality, and ease.

With your Peace Point guiding you and systems in place, you're no longer running on fumes; you're growing with purpose.

Just by reading this book, you are already embodying the life-first CEO identity.

> **Reflection Box**
>
> When I started this journey, I believed ____. Now, I believe ____.

Redefining PEACE & Profit On Your Own Terms

It's not about doing more. It's about doing what matters most.

PEACE and profit are now yours to define.

You're free to design your business around your life, not the other way around. That might mean:

- honoring your energy,
- pricing for your capacity,
- saying no with confidence,
- or taking rest or unplugged time without guilt.

You have a system that helps you think less about what's hard and trust more in what's aligned.

When you lead with this energy and strategic clarity, the ripple effect is real.

It starts close to home. Your family notices the shift—more presence, less stress. Your kids see a model of what it looks like to build with both ambition and boundaries. Your clients feel the difference in how you show up. Your team is steadier under your leadership.

And from there, the ripples spread wider. Your community sees that it's possible to grow without grinding yourself down. Other women see that they, too, can give themselves permission to define their own enough.

That's how this work multiplies—one aligned decision at a time.

When women have both money and peace, the world changes— starting at home.

You don't just create profit; you become a model of peace and power.

Create Your 90-Day Peace Plan

Picture this: It's a Monday morning, and you're reviewing your calendar with a coffee in hand—not with dread, but with calm. Your systems are humming, your energy is protected, and your week feels like it actually fits your life.

Ready to make it stick?

Choose one PEACE pillar—Profit, Energy, Alignment, Capacity, or Ease—to focus on for the next 90 days.

Go deep, not wide. Small, intentional steps will bring more lasting impact than trying to do it all at once.

Pick one habit or system to strengthen. Decide how you'll define success and how you want to feel.

And remember: small, imperfect steps still move you forward. You don't have to overhaul everything at once. The power is in showing up, even when it's messy.

Take your time. You don't need to rush. This is your plan. Make sure it reflects *your* vision of success.

You don't have to earn your enough through exhaustion. You get to define it through intention.

Reflection Box

What boundaries do I need to reinforce to stay in alignment?

What will I stop doing in the next 90 days?

Pause & Practice

1. Brain dump every goal or task related to each PEACE pillar
2. Circle the top two priorities
3. Start with one quick win, then build from there
4. Ask yourself: What does 'enough' look like in this season of life—and what's one way I can honor that this week?

Integration is a Cycle

Like the tide, some seasons will swell with energy, and others will pull you inward. Both are part of the rhythm.

When life happens:

- Pause and reflect
- Adjust your plan
- Focus on what matters now

In hard seasons, give yourself permission to pause and realign. This strategy is built to adapt with you. If something feels off, it's time to evolve.

Revisit the system quarterly. Let it grow with you.

This isn't about perfection. It's about presence. You're no longer avoiding the hard parts; you're meeting them with resilience.

And when you need help? Ask. Even CEOs need support.

Step Into Your Next-Level

You now:

- Understand your numbers
- Make confident spending and saving choices
- Talk about money without shame
- Model healthy financial habits for your family and clients
- Lead with clarity instead of chaos

You're not juggling everything; you're honoring what matters most.

Your legacy starts now.

> What legacy am I building, now that I'm leading from peace?

Need More Support?

If you're craving deeper support, you're not alone—and you don't have to figure it out by yourself.

Whether you want a single session or long term support, next steps are waiting when you are ready. You'll find details in the resources section or at thepeacestrategy.com.

Sometimes, support isn't about fixing. It's about being witnessed, affirmed, and guided back to your own wisdom.

You're not selfish for investing in PEACE—you're choosing to grow in a way that honors your life.

We can only go so far alone. Let's walk this next part together.

> *"You're not behind. You're building something that fits."*

You've built the foundation. You've chosen PEACE as your strategy.

And because of that, even when setbacks come, you'll have a way back to peace.

Because let's be real: life still happens. Old habits creep back in. Systems get tested. And sometimes, even when you know what works, you slip into what's familiar.

That doesn't mean you've failed—it just means you're human.

That's why next, we'll talk about what to do when setbacks hit—and how to keep moving forward without losing your peace.

CHAPTER 11

Common Pitfalls of The PEACE Strategy™

"Success is often found through failure"

Where This Gets Hard (and How to Keep Going)

You've built your PEACE rhythm. But let's be honest—life has a way of testing even the best systems.

Starting is hard, yes—but staying consistent? That's where the real growth happens.

And it won't always be neat. But messiness doesn't mean failure. It means you're learning. It means you're building resilience.

The moments when this feels hardest are often the ones showing you what needs your attention most. That's not a flaw; it's feedback.

The PEACE Strategy™ was built to adapt. It's flexible, not fixed. A rhythm, not a rulebook. And you're not meant to master it all at once.

Let's normalize what can throw you off and exactly how to recenter.

Pitfall #1: Trying to Do It All at Once

"I got overwhelmed and gave up."

Said every single client who tried to implement Profit First—or the entire PEACE framework—on their own.

Here's the trap: you start strong, fired up by excitement or pressure, and try to overhaul everything at once. It feels doable in the moment, but momentum without pacing always leads to burnout.

Ease in—don't overload yourself. You don't need to master all five pillars today. You just need to focus on one aligned pillar at a time, let it settle into your rhythm, and then add more when you are ready.

One of my favorite tools for this is what I call **The PEACE Reset**. Instead of trying to juggle everything, dedicate a week to recalibration:

- Day 1: Profit
- Day 2: Energy
- Day 3: Alignment
- Day 4: Capacity
- Day 5: Ease

Spend each day reviewing, adjusting, and setting one clear system or goal for the upcoming quarter. By Friday, you'll have clarity without overwhelm—and a plan that actually feels doable.

You can absolutely do this Reset on your own. And if you're the kind of person who thrives with accountability or fresh perspectives, this is also a beautiful thing to do with a coach, biz bestie, or trusted community.

You might feel like you're behind. You're not. You're building something sustainable.

Progress over perfection. Every step counts.

Pitfall #2: Ignoring Profit Because It Feels "Selfish"

"I still feel weird about paying myself."

On a group coaching call, a CEO shared how she handled profit sharing with her team. When her employees didn't meet their KPIs, she took the excess—not out of greed, but because she had carried the excess weight herself. She had built the business, upheld the vision, and filled the gaps. That moment reframed everything: claiming profit wasn't selfish. It was earned.

If money stirs guilt, you're not alone. We've inherited stories that say rich = greedy. Especially for women.

Some women even struggle with earning more than their partner. Or feeling like success means they have to do more for others to "justify" it.

But here's the truth: profit is how your business sustains you. It's not selfish—it's smart leadership.

Start small: even a tiny auto-transfer into your personal account is a beginning.

Pay yourself like the CEO you are. Your business isn't a job—it's your freedom engine.

You're not greedy—you're grounded.

Pitfall #3: Letting Old Capacity Habits Creep In

"I said yes to too much again."

This is the one I still struggle with the most—especially when scarcity creeps in or tax season looms. I catch myself estimating timelines as if I'm doing everything myself, forgetting I have a capable team. I overpromise because I don't want to disappoint anyone. People-pleaser in recovery, right here.

This one sneaks up. You're feeling good, so you say yes. You overfill your calendar, then suddenly the house is a mess, you're behind on invoices, and you're running on fumes.

This isn't failure. It's a sign to pause and recalibrate.

> **Check in:**
> - Am I rushing through my days?
> - Am I resenting what I said yes to?
> - Am I reacting instead of leading?
>
> If the answer is yes to any, it's time to realign.

Go back to your ideal schedule. Reinforce boundaries. Choose one thing to cut this week. Your future self will thank you.

Rest isn't a reward. It's a requirement.

Pitfall #4: Avoiding Your Numbers Again

"I just... stopped looking."

Many entrepreneurs didn't start their businesses to become bookkeepers. I've had countless clients tell me they're 'allergic to numbers'—not because they lack intelligence, but because traditional finance tools felt cold, confusing, or even shaming. The pressure to know everything, paired with past experiences or beliefs about money, can make even opening a spreadsheet feel overwhelming.

You're not alone. Numbers fatigue is real, especially if your financial history carries shame or anxiety.

When it gets heavy, we avoid it. But PEACE isn't avoidance—it's awareness.

Come back gently:

- Start with your Peace Point.
- Look at just the past 30 days.
- Celebrate one small win.

You don't need to know everything right now. You just need to know where you are and where you are going.

PEACE doesn't punish. It invites you back.

Pitfall #5: Treating PEACE Like a One-Time Fix

"I thought I was done after I finished the book!"

The PEACE Strategy™ isn't a one-and-done checklist. It's a rhythm to return to again and again.

One of my clients emailed me a few months after our session and said, "I really thought I had it figured out until everything got busy again." She hadn't failed. Life had just shifted.

When we went through the PEACE pillars again, she saw exactly what needed to be tweaked, and she felt immediate relief.

I love Brooke Weinstein's "Rule of Threes"—a reminder that your nervous system often needs 3 seconds, 3 minutes, 3 hours, or even 3 days, 3 weeks, or 3 months to regulate and rewire.

The same goes for integrating new rhythms like the PEACE Strategy™. You might *understand* it quickly, but embodying it? That takes time. So if you find yourself slipping back into old habits or feeling overwhelmed, don't panic—just come back to the PEACE Strategy™.

Change doesn't happen all at once, and that's okay. The key is staying with it gently, with grace, and letting each cycle bring you back to center.

Just like your needs shift with the seasons, so does your business. Some quarters might focus on Capacity. Others on Profit. While some seasons, the only focus will be rest.

Make it part of your routine. Revisit it quarterly. Adjust, refine, and celebrate.

Consistency isn't perfection. It's the reward.

Pause & Practice

Your Gentle Reset

Pick one pitfall you recognize in yourself. Then reflect:

- What might be one gentle way to recenter this week?
- What boundary or belief could help me realign?
- What's one small win I've already had with the PEACE Strategy™?

Write it down. Speak it aloud. Share it with someone. Let this be your nudge back into alignment—not a scolding, but a soft place to begin again.

> **Reflection Box**
>
> When I fall into old habits, I will remind myself that...
> The one shift I can make this week to return to peace is...
> Progress looks like...

A Small Win

One client was following her system but still feeling like she wasn't making enough. When she finally opened her QuickBooks, she realized she'd made more and saved more than she thought—and that single moment gave her the confidence to pay herself more for the first time in a year. It wasn't perfect. But it was enough to remind her she was capable—and that was all she needed to keep going.

Progress, Not Perfection

You will mess up. That doesn't mean you've failed.

The difference between a business that burns you out and one that brings you back to yourself is knowing how to come back and keep going—that's resilience.

So, when you feel off track:

- Return to your Peace Point.
- Revisit your calendar.

- Check in with your energy.
- Reconnect to your aligned vision.
- Look at your ease systems.

This isn't about doing more. It's about doing what matters.

You don't need to prove anything. You just need to return to what works for you.

You didn't fall off track. You're finding your way back. And that's the point.

Every time you come back, you strengthen your rhythm—and your ripple effect spreads.

Because resilience isn't about never slipping. It's about knowing how to return—again and again.

And when you do, the people closest to you feel it. That's how your work multiplies—one aligned comeback at a time.

Next, let's revisit what "enough" means—and what lies beyond it.

☑ PEACE Pitfall Reset Table

Use this as your check-in guide when things feel off. Start where you recognize yourself, and return gently.

Pitfall	What It Sounds Like	Your Gentle Reset
1. Trying to Do It All at Once	"I got overwhelmed and gave up."	One pillar. One habit. Let it settle first.
2. Ignoring Profit Because it Feels "Selfish"	"I still feel weird about paying myself."	Start small. Auto-transfer $25. You are worthy.
3. Letting Old Capacity Habits Creep In	"I said yes to too much again."	Cut one thing this week. Boundaries = peace.
4. Avoiding Your Numbers Again	"I just...stopped looking."	Start with 30 days. Celebrate one small win.
5. Treating PEACE Like a One-Time Fix	"I thought I was done after I finished the book!"	Revisit quarterly. This is a rhythm not a race.

CHAPTER 12

Finding Your Enough—and Building Beyond It

Enough isn't the ceiling. It's the foundation.

Once you know how to come back, the next question is: where are you coming back to?

That's where your enough becomes the anchor.

What is "Enough" Really?

When I ask women how much money they want to make, the first answer is often, "A million dollars."

My next question? "Why?"

That's when the conversation gets quiet.

Wanting a million is fine! Dreaming big means you're honoring your vision. But let's be honest: do you have a plan for that money? Are you ready to lead at that level?

What we really need to define first is your *enough—from your Peace Point back in Chapter Two.* Not based on cultural narratives. Not based on comparison. Based on *you*.

Ask yourself:

- What does my rich life actually look like? Maybe it's weekly date nights and no weekend work. Or a $5k annual vacation fund. Or working 25 hours a week, max.
- What am I spending on each month?
- What am I saving for?
- What do I splurge on with joy?
- How do I give or invest?
- What's my time worth?

Put a number to that life—not the dream of "more," but the vision that truly fuels you. That number is your *enough*.

Think of your enough as your peace point for your future self.

You might land at $300k, $80k, or even $1 million—or even bigger. It's valid either way. But chasing someone else's dream will dim your light and fast-track you to burnout.

The idea that we always need more? That's a cultural lie.
You don't need more—you need your enough.

Enough isn't about settling—it's about anchoring. It's your North Star. From this grounded place, you'll:

- Know when to say yes
- Feel confident saying no
- Recognize alignment when it arrives

When I first started my business, my *enough* was $2,000/month with the ability to stay home with my son. That was perfect for our season. As life evolved, so did our enough—and that's the point. Growth is allowed AND so is simplicity.

A client of mine once came in aiming for multi-six figures because "everyone" said that was the mark of success. But when we walked through her actual life priorities—flexibility, time with her aging parents, and enough to travel multiple times a year—her true enough was $60k. Once she saw that, her whole energy shifted. She stopped chasing, started designing, and actually hit her number faster with PEACE.

> **Reflection Box**
>
> What does "enough" look like for me in this season?
>
> What would it feel like to honor that fully?

What Comes After Enough

"When your needs are met, your vision expands."

Reaching enough doesn't mean you stop dreaming—it means you get to dream from a place of peace, not panic.

You get to enjoy the extra and settle in your cozy, peaceful lifestyle.

The PEACE Strategy™—Profit, Energy, Alignment, Capacity, and Ease—is your path to building a business that honors both your ambition *and* your well-being.

From here you can:

- Track your profit
- Protect your energy
- Align your work with your values
- Honor your capacity
- Operate with ease

You build beyond enough when it feels *aligned,* not because you feel behind.

> If you didn't have to prove anything, what would you build next?

Pause & Practice

Close your eyes and imagine your business fully aligned with your version of enough.

- What does your calendar look like?
- Who are you working with?
- How do you feel at the end of each day?

Write it down.

PEACE as a Legacy

"Your presence is the legacy."

One morning, I told my son, "Have fun today." He smiled and said, "I always have fun, Mama." That moment hit me hard, in the best way. He knew joy was normal. He knew I was present. That's legacy.

Entrepreneurship gives us a chance to model something new for our families:

- That rest is sacred
- That money is a conversation, not a secret
- That leadership includes softness, not just grit

Talk to your kids about saving for shared goals. Let them see you make value-aligned purchases. Show them what financial clarity and emotional peace look like in action.

One client started including her kids in her money check-ins. At first, it felt awkward. But soon, it became a family ritual—reviewing goals, celebrating small wins, and deciding on one thing to save for together. Her kids began to see money not as a source of stress, but as a tool for freedom and joy. That's the ripple effect.

It extends beyond your home. It shapes your clients, your community, your industry. Legacy isn't just about big wins—it's about intentional presence.

Being family-first isn't small. It's revolutionary.

If you want a cozy, life-honoring business instead of a chaotic empire, that's valid. And if someday your cozy business evolves into an empire because it feels aligned? That's beautiful, too.

Lead with PEACE. Let your values drive your growth.

> **Ways to Keep Going**
>
> You've redefined success, reclaimed your time, and connected deeply with your own version of enough. Now, it's time to keep that momentum—sustainably.
>
> The PEACE Strategy™ works best when you come back to it again and again. You can absolutely do this on your own—but you don't have to. If you're ready for more support, here are three ways we can keep going:
>
> - **Clarity Call** —A focused 90-minute reset to untangle the numbers, refine your pricing, or realign your next steps.
> - **VIP Day** — A deep-dive strategy day to map your offers, systems, and money plan—so you leave with a clear, custom action plan.
> - **Ongoing Partnership** — Longer-term support to help you anchor PEACE into every area of your business and sustain your growth with clarity and calm.
>
> No matter which path you choose, the goal is the same: *more clarity, more profit, more peace—and a business that loves you back.*

You've named your enough. You've seen how the PEACE Strategy™ carries you toward it—and beyond it, when it feels aligned.

This isn't about chasing someone else's dream. It's about creating your own.

You have enough. You are enough.

And now, you're building something even better.

With PEACE as your guide, we'll land this journey with clarity and calm—because this has never just been about building a business. It's about building a life rooted in money, peace, and a ripple effect that lasts.

CONCLUSION

You've made it to the end, but really, this is your beginning.

When you create PEACE in your business, you find alignment—not just with your work, but with your family, your energy, and your values.

You're present for T-ball games and dance recitals without guilt or the mental to-do list running in the background. You have a plan. You know your priorities. You know your worth.

My hope is that you're saying to yourself:
"I didn't know how much I needed this."
"This actually feels doable."
"I'm not broken. I just needed a better plan."

That's the truth—you were never broken.

This isn't about doing more. It's about doing what matters in a way that fits your life. The PEACE Strategy™ is proof that profit and peace can coexist—that you can lead your business with confidence without sacrificing yourself in the process.

You've done the mindset work, the financial work, and the most important work of all: learning to trust yourself again.

You're the CEO now. And you've earned every bit of that title.

> **Final Reflection Box**
>
> - Where were you when you picked up this book?
> - What stories did you believe about money, success, or your worth?
> - What surprised you most about this process?
> - How are you showing up differently in your business and in your life?
> - How do you now define peace and profit for yourself?
> - What patterns are you ready to release for good?
> - What new belief are you most proud of embracing?
> - What legacy do you want to model—at home, in business, and in how you show up?

The Ripple Effect in Action

One of my clients closed her laptop one Friday afternoon and picked up her daughter from school. It wasn't a vacation day. It was just her new normal. She'd used this framework to reduce her client load, implement profit-first payouts, and start taking every Friday off—without losing income. Her daughter said, "I love Fridays with you, Mommy." That's the ripple effect.

Another client had never felt comfortable talking about money—not with her clients, not with her partner, and definitely not with herself.

After using her Peace Point and setting up a personal paycheck system, she gave herself her first raise in two years and began having monthly financial check-ins with her partner. "I don't dread those conversations anymore. We're building something together now."

As for me? My success is in the little things: hiking with my dogs, skiing when the powder hits, traveling with family, or simply watching my son giggle. It's having open space on my calendar for creativity. It's being present in my own body.

Even on hard days, I'm reminded why I started. Because I don't have to do it like everyone else to succeed. And neither do you.

Revisit, Reflect, Recenter

Whenever you feel off track, come back to your **Peace Point.** Come back to **Energy, Alignment, Capacity, and Ease.** PEACE will always be here as your compass—ready to guide you back to what matters most.

Keep a sticky note with your favorite pillar on your laptop. Set a calendar reminder to revisit your 90-day Peace Plan. Make space for the questions that help you course correct—not because you're off track, but because life evolves and you will, too.

Balance isn't about perfection. It's about building the systems that support you when life gets messy.

If You're Craving More Support

Sometimes, the fastest way forward isn't doing it alone—it's walking with someone who believes in your vision as much as you do. Whether it's a clarity call, a VIP day, or a longer partnership, I'd be honored to walk that next leg of the journey with you.

Here's what one client said after we wrapped a VIP Day together:

"I finally feel like I can breathe. I know what to do next. And for the first time in a long time, I believe I can do it."

And finally—thank you. Thank you for reading, for showing up, and for daring to believe your business could be different. Writing this book was for women like you—the ones building not just businesses, but lives worth living.

I'm so proud of you for choosing this path—for yourself, your family, and your legacy.

You've got this. Keep coming back to what matters. Keep refining. Keep resting. Keep rising.

Remember:

- **Profit** — pays you.
- **Energy** — sustains you.
- **Alignment** — anchors you.
- **Capacity** — protects you.
- **Ease** — supports you.

This is your clear path to a business that loves you back.

Your peace is powerful. Your presence is your legacy.

And your next chapter? It's yours to write.

REFERENCES

Garton, Eric. "What Makes Entrepreneurs Burn Out." Harvard Business Review, April 18, 2018. https://hbr.org/2018/04/what-makes-entrepreneurs-burn-out

Housel, Morgan. The Psychology of Money. Harriman House, 2020.

Michalowicz, Mike. Profit First. Portfolio, 2017.

Ruta, Kelly. The Subconscious Millionaire Program.

Tiffan, Lauren. "The Mental Health Crisis in Entrepreneurship." Entrepreneurs' Center. 1, May. 2023.

Travis, Michelle. "3 Ways That Gender Bias Fuels Employee Burnout In Women." Forbes. 25, Feb. 2025. https://www.forbes.com/sites/michelletravis/2025/02/25/3-ways-that-gender-bias-fuels-employee-burnout-in-women/

RESOURCES

Resources to Support Your PEACE Journey

Tools

PEACE & Profit Starter Kit — Guided workbook, audio lessons, and templates to help you apply the PEACE Strategy faster.

Get instant access at thepeacestrategy.com

If you're ready for deeper support, I'd love to walk alongside you.

- 90-Minute Profit & Clarity Call — One focused session for quick wins.
- VIP Day — A full-day deep dive into your offers, pricing, and systems.
- Long term support (6 or 12 months) — Ongoing strategy & support for women ready to scale with peace and profit at the center.

Explore all options at <u>thepeacestrategy.com/</u>

thepeacestrategy.com

ABOUT THE AUTHOR

Kayla Caldwell is the creator of the PEACE Strategy™, a Profit First strategist, a financial coach, and the founder of KC Virtual Bookkeeping.

A former bookkeeper turned business mentor, Kayla helps service-based women entrepreneurs feel confident with their money and build businesses that support their lives—not consume them. Her bold, family-first approach to business finances helps women pay themselves well, protect their energy, and lead with clarity—without shame or spreadsheet-induced headaches.

In 2025, she was named one of Insightful Accountant's **Top 25 Up & Coming QuickBooks ProAdvisors**. But what matters most to her isn't titles—it's seeing women who once felt "bad with money" realize they were never broken. They just needed the right framework and support.

Through her offers—from quick clarity sessions to deep-dive partnerships—Kayla walks alongside women as they reimagine their finances, redesign their schedules, and reclaim their worth. She's known for her bold but compassionate mantra: *profit isn't selfish—it's smart.*

Outside of her work, Kayla is a mom, wife, skier, and former TV meteorologist. She believes in early-morning coffee, constant learning, fresh powder days, and showing up for what matters most.

This is her first book—but it was written with hundreds of women in mind, and thousands more to come. Because Kayla isn't just here to help you "get your numbers right." She's here to help you reclaim your **profit, your PEACE, and your presence**—so your business finally loves you back.

- 📍 [www.kcvirtualbookkeeping.com]
- 📧 [support@kcvirtualbookkeeping.com]
- 📱 [@thepeacestrategy on Instagram]

www.ingramcontent.com/pod-product-compliance
Lightning Source LLC
Chambersburg PA
CBHW050112170426
43198CB00014B/2546